THE VOICE OF ORION

Ernest L. Norman

As the clairvoyant channel for the Spiritual Unarius, he bears the marks of psychic stigma, called the "Eye of Mohammed" which during transmissions becomes activated into the raised circular welt caused by energy beams projected from the Higher Planes.

THE

VOICE OF ORION

Clairvoyantly Received

BY

Ernest L. Norman

The Fourth Volume of

THE PULSE OF CREATION

Published By
UNARIUS, SCIENCE OF LIFE
P.O. Box 1042
El Cajon. Calif. 92020

THE VOICE OF ORION

© Copyright 1961

By

Unarius Educational Foundation

Printed in China

ISBN 0-9724710-0-6

Third Edition

*

UNARIUS
UNiversal ARticulate Interdimensional
Understanding of Science

PREFACE

Once again the time has come to present to the earnest Truth seeker one more volume in the "Pulse of Creation" series; and just as in all similar presentations, we do so with a certain sense of justifiable pride and a feeling of accomplishment; for not only have overwhelming obstacles been overcome in various technical aspects—thanks to the persistence and dedication of Ruth and Velma—in such problems as transcribing, editing, setting up the copy for the press, etc., but also that these books and other liturgies as a whole, represent the combined efforts of the Great Spiritual Organization of Unarius which has been in the making for thousands of years, and is now culminating in this final stage of expression.

In this respect it should be noted that during the comparatively few years in which Unarius has had its first present day earth world beginnings, much has been accomplished and already many thousands of wonderful testimonials have been safely filed away for future reference; when at any convenient time they

can be brought forth to prove the miraculous effica-
ciousness of this interdimensional science, as well as
to give great inspiration to those who are trying to
solve the maze of differences in their own lives; and
also to obtain tangible and evidential proof of the evolutionary continuity of life.

No doubt these and other testimonials give great
joy to the many advanced Spiritual Personalities who
are laboring so assiduously to the cause of Unarius.
In the future years yet to come, many more glorious
chapters will be written in the hearts and lives of
those who will come to know Unarius—as the full
justification of all, long-sought after emancipations,
the fulfillment of their greatest hopes and aspira-
tions; and most important of all, to begin their own
development into one of those oft-portrayed angelic
figures.

No doubt, too, many others aside from the ardent
Truth seekers will find a great answer in Unarius; the
scientist of the future will find in these works definite
clues, descriptions and other necessary data wherein
he can propound the beginnings of his new interdimensional science. The doctor and psychiatrist also
will find the answer to many age-old mysteries of life;
the riddle of incurable diseases will be solved for all
time, and our present day hospitals and prisons
could become relics of the past just as would the
impedimenta of the great armies and navies now in
use.

Generally speaking, however, perhaps it may be
that the larger portion of mankind will never find any
semblance of an Utopian existence on this planet
earth world; for as it has been conceived, the earth
may always remain largely a place where—just as in

other similar earth worlds—mankind takes his first step in climbing the ladder into immortality. Yet there are those, too, who are still among the first strugglers who would take their second step; and it is for these souls that Unarius is so dedicated.

Therefore, as you read this and other books of Unarius, it is sincerely hoped for and desired that you are among those desiring the next step, and that you will find all the necessary answers, equivalents, and transcending power to enable you to find the next rung on the unending ladder into Infinity.

E. L. Norman

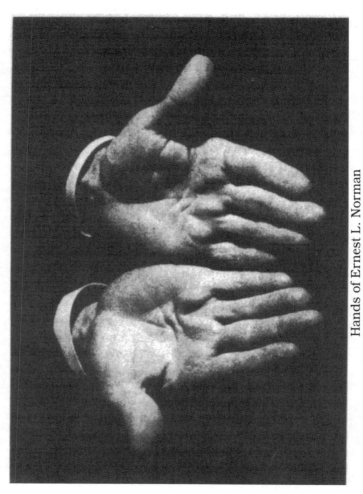

Hands of Ernest L. Norman

Showing the psychic stigmata of the nail hole scars which appeared psychically within 5 days time, upon re-living and experiencing, mentally and psychically, his experience of the Holy Land episode when he was crucified.

CHAPTER 76

A very special welcome and greeting to you dear ones, from a new and different section of Shamballa. For personal reasons of identification, I shall come to you as Athena. I am somewhat very closely related, in a spiritual way, with several forces which are in existence on the earth at this time. It was through one of these spiritual forces that I first came in contact with the necessary personages who will enable us to explore this dimension of the seven Shamballas. We shall present, in our way, something in the nature of spiritual interpretations to enlarge your concepts in the fields which are relative to teaching, and to find new paths of truth and wisdom which will further synthesize these concepts into your everyday philosophy.

The planet to which we are to go at the present moment, for reasons of identification, we have called Orion. In the winter season, if you look into the skies, you will see the ancient mythological figure of the warrior, Orion, and that he appears to be holding aloft a sword in somewhat of a forward position. A closer inspection of this figure will reveal two triangles which are formed by the right arm and by the leg; and around his middle portion is a belt of very beautiful stars. A somewhat similar interpretation could be that he is holding aloft a torch.

Approaching this planet directly at an incredible rate of speed beyond that of light, you will see it has its own characteristic frequency, which you will interpret in your sense of color, as being a beautiful golden yellow. We are coming directly in contact with a great city of expression, which we are calling Helianthus, inasmuch as it represents the form of a sunflower, with its thirty-three petals stemming from a great central section. These thirty-three petals are the spiritual interpretation of the expression or concept of the thirty-three Logi, who are ruling the celestial and spiritual dimensions with which we are now immediately associated.

In the future developments of the different transmissions and in the exploration through this city, you will find it is, like the other centers, one of a very beautiful and spiritual nature. The expressions of life found in this center are of the same nature which you have found before; the buildings are the same beautiful crystal-like structures with which you have become familiar, since the basic nature of the expression is a spiritual one in these centers.

My own relationship in the teaching expression, and in other ways in which we interpret life here, is a more personal one in my linkage with the seventh section or the seventh expression. I may be called the biocentric polarity of one who, at your earth time, was called Zoroaster. In the future developments of the transmissions we shall get into the relationship of the biune or the biocentric consciousness, as it actually exists as the manifestation or the interchange of polarities and dimensions of energy transference, which has sometimes been called thought continuities of spiritual expression.

The old idea of sex, or man and woman, as you have so found it within your minds on the earth, is not in any sense of the word an interpretation which can be used in these higher dimensions. We have long since passed beyond the time when such concepts were relative in our expression in some terrestrial planet or plane. We have now evolved to a point where a true relationship with our opposite or diametrically opposed polarity is now assuming proportions which enable it to manifest itself as a personality in direction and in unison with the higher dimensions, in a way in which you yourself on the earth plane know nothing of the nature of these elements of idea, thought, and form as they are expressed from the inward or spiritual nature of man.

We are poised somewhere in space immediately above the great temple in this very beautiful center. As you look about you, you will notice this section of the great city can be likened somewhat to the heart of the sunflower. Here, the ornate temple is used in the various spiritual initiations, emergences, and ascensions, to and from these dimensions by the numerous Initiates, Adepts and Masters who so manifest themselves.

In the future transmissions, several persons connected with the expression of teaching and synthesis, and formerly known as the identities of Plato and Archimedes on earth, would like personally to give individual transmissions or help to conduct you through this center. You may wonder, since Archimedes and Plato were philosophers in your earth plane; but you must also remember that they, as well as many other Greek interpolators, gave their own academic expressions in the numerous ancient academies, for they were very popular during the Grecian or Hellenic Age.

The subject of man is in itself one of vital importance in your own immediate evolution in the generalities and in the ideas which were brought into your consciousness in the previous exploration of the planet Hermes and of the city of Aureleus. The numerous philosophical interpretations of mankind on the earth in the ancient and more recent times, as expressed in the different forms of music, art, poetry and literature—as they are contained in these histories—are of many and diverse expressions. We can say for the moment that the formula used by the German philosopher Hegel, in posing the thesis and antithesis, that man selected, in his own expression of life, the reactionary elements which best suited the function of the normal sequence of his daily living, as the general conclusions of these ideas or expressions of experience into a person's world and dimension related him to a definite personal concept or philosophy.

It was this synthesis which enabled the philosopher of a later day to become somewhat of a metaphysician, and thus he advanced into the more abstract concepts of man's nature, so that in his hypothesis, man was able to include in his physical dimension the objectivism of his own mind. Consequently, he had a definite relationship of expression within that dimension from the mind; and even his own body could be included as a direct result of his interpretations of life in that dimension. Philosophers have been wont to consider this physical dimension as something which exists within the realm or the concept of emotional experience, as it relates man to his own expression of life and has in itself a certain definite psychic impact.

We should never lose sight of the original objective or aim of the individual as is so contained in all of the universal concepts as they are woven or projected from the Mind of God. It is the innate knowledge and wisdom within man that relates him to the different dimensions of expression, for the purpose or intent of acquainting him with the rebuilding and revitalizing of his nature, to the point where he becomes a definite personal individual. He thus relates himself to the Infinite Mind of God in such a personal relationship, that he eventually becomes an integrated part of this Great Universal Mind of God.

As has been observed, there are definite trends or periods of evolution in the consciousness of man as he expresses himself collectively in an age of expression. We could take the Age of Reformation as an outstanding example, for it was an age of liberation in the thought and consciousness of man. Initiates from the higher astral and spiritual realms, including Shamballa, were reincarnated onto the earth, and they were thus able to interpolate their own ideas which were just beyond the boundary or the horizon of man's thinking in his own dimension in that era. Other factors are quite obvious, inasmuch as we would see that because these expressions and their personal creators contained influences from the pure spiritual dimensions, they were thus able to give to the world a much broader and more advanced concept.

Here again is a very intelligent relationship with God, one which is working in its own way with the harmonic conclusion of man in his numerous evolutions. The postulations of numerous theories which are beyond the immediate vision or horizon of man's inception or induction into his own way of life, are quite naturally, instantaneously rejected by the individual. It is this, his most instinctive and inborn nature, which enables him to select the necessary condiments of life which are most factual, and which will come into being as a more useful expression in his way of life. Remember that the innate nature of man, as it relates to his Higher Superconscious and indirectly to God Himself, must therefore, in its longings, return to its natural spiritual elements; for it was conceived or inducted into the material dimension purely for the purpose of experience. Experience in everyone's life must therefore be included and concluded within every possible realm and dimension of expansion, which the individual feels inclined to explore or to include in his life. The confining expressions, and the lack of selfhood in these expressions, very often react as does the lack of a safety valve on a steam engine, which quickly blows the boiler to bits. Thus the confining expressions of daily life, or the lack of individual expressions in man, can lead him into expressions of life or dimensions of thought which are very destructive and perverted.

The thought behind the inductive relationship of man with his higher self, gives rise to what has been called the libido or the drive in man. It assumes interest in all of the things about him, which enables him to partake of his daily life. This infusion of interest in the creative possibilities of his most inward nature, is the most redeeming and the most conclusive factor of man's evolution and reincarnation; and the continual reliving and experiencing of the processes of daily life, which include the termination of the different years in his terrestrial dimension, are, in themselves, constructive elements which enter into man's personality. It can be very easily seen that the conclusion of such constructive experiences are motivated by the forces which project him forward in his evolution.

Likewise, man inducting into his consciousness, experiences of a retrograde nature, can thereby retard his experiences into subastral dimensions, which become more and more destructive to his own nature and intent. Man never stands still; he is going either forward or backward. He is either progressing or retrogressing. It is this most dominant and vital concept within one's mind which will determine what he will be in a few thousand years from now; whether he will be a wandering entity, which is submerged in the blackness of his retarded condition, or whether he will be an illuminated soul ready to stand at the threshold of some higher spiritual dimension from which he has partaken unto himself the Radiance and the Brilliance of God's Innermost Nature. As has been mentioned, the experience itself is of no consequence. It is the value which is derived from such an experience, whether it is constructive or destructive to man's nature. That which remains will be a constructive or destructive element in some of the more immediate and future evolutions as a force which exists in his psychic body.

In some of the future transmissions we intend to give some very authoritative information in the fields of the sciences known on your earth as medicine and psychiatry. We wish to portray to you some of the damage which is done to the psychic centers of the individual by the injection and the partaking of the numerous drugs which are sedatives, or of an anesthetic nature. The drugs of anesthesia, as they are used in the hospitals, in the fields of surgery, and their effect upon the psychic nature of the individual will be explained in future transmissions in a manner which will be of great value in the future evolutions of man as he will live in the coming millennium.

As man vitally connects himself to the higher concepts of life, he will free himself from the very objective materialism which is at the present time destroying his civilization, and is placing mankind in general in a very decadent position. Life, as it exists for the average individual in your highly mechanized world today, is one which presents both numerous advantages and disadvantages, many of which were not known in a former age or dimension.

In the exploration of the previous histories of your earth, as you will see in the examination of life as it existed in the Age of the Reformation or the earlier ages of the Egyptian, Hindu, and Chinese civilizations, but especially in those of the immediate period of the Reformation, everyone, even the kings themselves and the noble ladies of the court, was trained in numerous capacities and trades. No one in those days who had any intelligence at all or who was capable of becoming a useful citizen in the capacity of such trades, neglected the opportunity to develop his talents.

Most of the elements of human life were made by hand, and so artifacted as direct expressions of the individual trade. They were expressed in the concepts of the numerous guilds, as they were called, which have their counterparts in the trade unions of your present day. However, the guilds in themselves were moral, rather than franchised, and, existing as they did in the moral consciousness, they consisted of democratic elements which were very highly evolved and humanitarian in nature. They endured purely through the essence and virtues of the character of the individual as he was included in these numerous guilds, or expressions of the trades and crafts, as they were expressed in those days. The noble ladies of the court, as I have said, would sit for many hours; and while they were gossiping about their neighbors, their fingers were busily plying the loom or the shuttle, and their needles were busily flying to construct garments or to embroider cloth with suitable designs and configurations which were both useful and pleasing to the eye.

Man in himself never becomes destructive or neurotic in his intent or purpose in any of his activities in such dimensions of expression, unless he becomes frustrated or thwarted in his natural desire for the expression of the constructive elements of his nature. Your present civilization is one which poses a very grave problem, not only of national but of international importance. The average individual, is so submerged with the artifacts and contrivances of the civilization about him, that he becomes something which has been likened to a robot, and consequently the individual portions of his spiritual consciousness and the desire to express himself constructively in a higher form, have been suppressed. They have been channeled into a more laborious element, which is very highly exploited in producing the numerous machinations of your present day civilization.

Thus man becomes someone who screws together some particular part of a machine on an assembly line, and by the end of the day he is too tired to do more than eat his meal and tumble into bed; so he very soon seeks an escape. He contrives a yearly vacation for a few days away, and in going on that vacation he becomes so involved in the process of trying to free himself in some escape mechanism, that he very often returns from the vacation to re-enter his normal life much more tired than he was before he went away. It is the continued reliving, the continued strife and turmoil within the individual which makes him tired and frustrated and eventually neurotic; yes, even psychotic. This may lead him into the attitude of the criminal, or into a state of apathy which is called by your psychiatrist, neurasthenia, or he may suffer a premature death from what is termed hypertension.

A drive through the suburban areas in many of the

sections of your country will display great tracts of homes; and although they are laid out rather neatly in long rows with paved streets in between, yet they portray—to a large degree—the continual repetitious sequence of life as it is expressed in your present civilization. Although these tracts of homes may embody several different exteriors, or they may have somewhat different interior arrangements yet they are all basically the same, and were given birth with the idea of exploiting and machinating the masses of people.

There are none of the more advanced concepts of life existing for the average tradesman or the businessman in your present civilization. There are no individual concepts and no liberations into the higher capacities of man's mind whereby he can go beyond the sham and tinsel of the everyday life about him. There is by far too much commercialism. However, at this time, I do not want to convey the impression that we are at all critical of your daily living. We are merely pointing out these things to you on the basis that the comparisons will enable mankind to integrate these concepts more realistically into their daily lives which will be of much greater value to them.

The idea of peace of mind, as it is contained in the individual, is a Utopian condition which, if he would evolve into, would mean something of the concept of destruction. If man ever did assume a position which was without blemish and without fault in his everyday expression, or if he arrived at such a time and place in which problems no longer existed, life would flow beautifully about him. If all he had to do was to reach out on an endless table, effortlessly, to snatch portions of everything he desired, such a condition would very quickly plunge him into an atrophied condition of mind. The body would also become very retrogressive in nature. The innate being of man and his evolution is so contrived and conceived in the Infinite Creation, that these obstacles, or problems, are seemingly placed in the pathway of the individual. These conditions must be surmounted or circumvented in an intelligent fashion and in such a relationship, that they will be of some real value and consequence to man in strengthening the moral fiber and tissue of his own character.

Because we are somewhat dependent in the relationship of vibration to you there on the earth, we hope that in the future, the conditions—universal, solar or otherwise—will be of a nature which will give us a more ready and free transmission of words and facts into your dimension. Until such future moments of contact, we again send our rays of love to you.

CHAPTER 77

Greetings, dear ones. I may in the future be identified as Kuthumi. I see that you are staggering somewhat under the impact of a new surprise, for you find yourself directly here in the second section of Parhelion.

In the previous and opening transmission, you were conducted by Athena to the planet of Orion and to the city of Helianthus. We here are always trying to keep the interest in these transmissions going by the element of personal surprise. Now, before we go into these explorations more fully and conduct you through these remaining sections—although you may think that much of this is seemingly repetitious—yet for the sake of clarification, I shall again interject the original concepts of Shamballa.

The Shamballas are divided into seven dimensional segments, each related not only to the history of evolution of man on your earth, but also to the numerous other astral and terrestrial planets of the cosmic universe. There is, as has been somewhat explained to you, a great deal of intercourse between the different spiritual centers existing in this great cosmic universe, called either a terrestrial or a spiritual cosmos and containing a vast number of planets, not only in the universe with which you are familiar from the picturization in the books and astronomical libraries of your world, but many of which you have not yet learned. This universe is like many others,

706

stemming from some great radial vortex of Celestial and Infinite Energy. It is quite natural that in the spiritual centers, since man is universal, and living as he does in the countless and innumerable dimensions—both terrestrial and spiritual—there must be a great deal of intercourse between these different relationships.

So it is that man truly evolves, and in the different elements of personal evolution, he more fully relates himself to his Infinite inception and conception from the Mind of God. Here, as in other sections of Parhelion, you will find the portrayal of life as it is expressed in the different dimensions on your earth, which may be likened to the museums, art galleries and the various other places where masses of materials are collected for the purpose of comparing values and their relationship to the different sciences, philosophies and inspirational arts of music, literature, and drama. The other centers are so constructed that they contain great galleries from which the student and teacher can more fully expound and relate his concepts into his own mind and for his own personal development.

It can be said that I spent a lifetime upon your planet, living in a very distant evolution of Chinese history. I also expressed something of the original conception and inception of Shamballa, as it was lived on the earth many hundreds of thousands of years ago. A little further along we shall go into other relationships which are called biocentric.

The student of truth who progresses in the different conceptions of philosophy, whether they are metaphysical, spiritual, or whatever classification to which they are related, will find that his universe expands about him. He will also find that the problems of mankind and the various evolutions of man's consciousness, are as numerous and infinite in number as his own. Because he is a creature of infinite conception, man must use a good deal of patience, and the elements of time and space must be conclusively eliminated from the consciousness of the individual before the true progressive relationship enters into his life. He must ever be ready and willing to believe in the Infinite Nature and Creation of all those things which may enter into his life; consequently, he will be in the pursuance of the diversified ways of his own evolution, so that he, too, shall become infinite in nature. Any individual who has so ascended by the direct will of his own mind, by his willingness, has integrated the will of God into this concept.

Man has progressed into the centers here in Parhelion only through the virtue, dominion, and will of his own consciousness. He has become neither great nor small, but has become only a better servant to his God and to his fellow man. The various and conflicting elements of life, in the different terrestrial planets in the beginning of man's evolution in some of the lower concepts, poses an infinite number and variety of interpretations.

As has been pointed out in previous transmissions, such varieties of interpretations to which man relates himself, pose in themselves as diametrical opposites. Here again we must stress emphatically the concept that as man is conceived in the spiritual nature, and as he so expresses himself in the lower dimensions, the same opposites of polarity which are sometimes conceived in the biocentric concept, are also expressed in his own individual concept. He has thus become quadrocentric in his own way. This quadrocentricity in turn will likewise lead into different dimensions and various versions of his expression, so that he is constantly influenced and impounded by the succession of these different interlinking harmonic factors into his interpretation of life in his daily way of living.

Before going into the actual exploration of this center, I would like to give you a little more of the working order and harmony of evolution as it is expressed in these spiritual dimensions. The one who is personified as Lord Buddha in the earth philosophies became one of the Council of Twelve, about one hundred years ago, during which time I served in the capacity as head director, or, as you call it, the executive or president of this section of Shamballa. The Buddha himself (and I am referring to the Guatama), is one of the existing Council of Twelve, just as are the other seven Avatars who previously gave their lives in service on your earth at different times. The one called Jesus, is at the present time, serving not only as one of the head executives, or the director over the Shamballas, but He is also in an active position in the Council of Twelve, which connects them with the thirty-three Lords, or Logi, as they are sometimes called. I am giving you this information simply to acquaint you with the fact that we, too, have a great deal of semblance and order in our dimensions, in consequence of our knowledge and understanding and our work with the general brotherhood of man in our capacity to evolve into more efficient outlets of this servitude and expression, if I can use the word "service" loosely.

The actual expression of life, as it exists with us, is one which means life itself in the expression of our service to our fellow man. We should at all times be able to function in unity and harmony with the expression as it flows into our consciousness from the higher dimensions, and this is expressed likewise in the different dimensions which we will say are below us; thus all evolve and grow into higher and into larger dimensional concepts of relationships.

The section here in Parhelion, which comes under the division of education and synthesis, has on its faculty of regular teachers, personages of the ancient Grecian, Egyptian, and Brahmanistic theosophies and expressions of the earth. There are numerous individuals who are personified as the Yogis, or the advanced Initiates of the different epochs and generations of time in the histories of the earth. There are others whose names would mean nothing to you as their evolutions have been confined in other portions of the terrestrial and cosmic universes. However, we do have one class here which is regularly conducted in the academy and is headed by Plato. If conditions are suitable, he will personally conduct you in a tour through his classroom and other sections of Parhelion. There is another philosopher and scientist here by the name of Archimedes, who is also teaching something of the relationship of the philosophies and sciences in the different dimensions. He, too, is very much interested in being of some assistance in the future expressions within the pages of the book which you are compiling.

Personally, I am the type of person who likes to go directly to the point and could never have been accused of being a loquacious person. Because these dimensions here in Parhelion and the classrooms and various functional orders have been quite clearly explained in different portions of the book, I shall not waste time here by further explaining these things to you.

This great center of Parhelion exists in somewhat of a higher vibratory rate, than the other six sections of the Shamballas, because Parhelion itself expresses a great directive force, since its position is immediately above. Although I dislike the word "above," we need to use these words to convey to you the differences in frequency transmission, or the way in which the different orders of dimensions are divided into the conscious expression of man in his different evolutions.

Entering the main portal, or doorway, of this section of Parhelion is somewhat similar to entering the other centers. Here you will immediately be confronted by a very beautiful fountain of pure energy which is in somewhat of a large circular courtyard. The ceiling, as it rises in rather a high and arched fashion, is composed of the endless, ceaseless, and pulsating energies of the Great Celestial Universe which seems to form a canopy above. The ceiling itself is constructively proportioned to contain many prisms, and because these are properly focused, they function by bringing into harmonic and corrective relationship, the different frequency spectrums of these energies, in order that the various personages who pass up and down the corridor and through the great central portico or courtyard, will thus be energized and conditioned in such a way that they can more readily associate and absorb the energies and projections of mind intelligences, which they encounter in their various activities.

This conditioning process is universal throughout the other sections, and is a very important fact which I would like to interject and point out to you. You may thus better understand the difference in the relationship of these sections to mankind in general, when an individual comes as an Initiate, or an Adept, or a Master into these sectional orders.

You will recall that in Coralanthea you saw Master Bach, a Master of music on the earth, teaching a definite relationship of chord structures in the chromatic scale, to numerous students who come to study music. Now again you will see other Masters who were formerly engaged on earth in musical activities, teaching music here in a slightly different relationship. Here, as in the fifth section of Parhelion, music becomes a therapeutic science, interjected into the fields of correcting the human body or the spiritual elements of the psychic body. Music does have a very definite therapeutic value in the corrective therapies of the bodies of mankind.

In this section, we shall explore music and its relationship in educational ways into other dimensions of man's consciousness. Music manifests in different ways as harmonic structures, existing within the personality of every human being. So likewise must other inspirational arts and their expressions be interwoven or fashioned. These various spectrums of vibrationary frequencies are so interwoven that they become definite spiritual elements which enable man to progress on up into a higher dimension. A man cannot be devoid of any of these seven different dimensional expressions, and expect to develop a spiritual personality sufficiently to enable him to progress into the higher dimensions. A person must develop a sense of harmonic relationship which is contained, not only in the field of music, but in the field of science. However, he must also obtain an understanding of relationship structures in the portrayal of words, as they are intoned in the cabalistic intonations of the human voice. He must learn of the other factors and elements as they are expressed from these centers, which must enter into the fabric and composition of his nature. This will make him, in his entirety, a human soul who can further progress into the higher dimensions of relationship.

In the various expressions of life philosophies contained in the earth dimensions, the elemental values are of the more emotional nature. Man, in such dimensions, is incapable of a pure and constructive expression of thought, when the various virtues or elements in his daily life are constructed of the emotional values, causing the psychic impact of experiences, as it was most properly presented to you previously. The inflections of the various experiences in the domain of emotional experience thus project themselves as definite wave forms into the psychic body of the individual, and will thus enable him further to construct and constitute himself into other dimensions of relationship. This may enable you to better understand why it is that many times an individual may be desirous of obtaining some of the various elements of life which are about him, only to find that in the possession and the acquisition of these different elements, he loses interest in them. He will also find that the ideas or philosophies which earlier were very important to him may at the moment lose their importance in comparison to different ideas and philosophies.

The word which I would like to interject here into your domain of consciousness is balance. We cannot over-emphasize the importance and value of balance in your everyday life. As you will thus see, your lives are constantly being projected from one polarity to another, or, as you have termed it, from the positive to the negative. Or, you may say that whenever you try to do something good, you always end up by having something bad happen to you. As has been explained, this is the diametrically opposed opposite or polarity of your everyday life. The balance which should be maintained, is somewhere in the position of relationship between the elements of the negative and the positive, formulating in your own minds, and acquiring as your daily philosophies, the proper relationship of these different polarities of the negative and positive. Thus you will acquire the necessary intelligence and fortitude which will enable you to progress into different relationships.

The idea that time and circumstance, or the age in which you live, is impinged into your consciousness, is somewhat unrelative. A person cannot be said to be standing still in any one dimension, or time; only by his own will and dominion, can this be. In a broad and overall sense, in an understanding of reincarnation and evolution, you place yourself in your own dimension and in your own time, as a direct purpose and intent of your own will. It could not be otherwise, for you have thus linked within your mind and within the psychic structures of your body, the factors which enable you to exist in your present circumstances. So it will be in your future evolutions. This fact is of the utmost importance, and one which must be remembered by the student of Truth, no matter in what circumstances he finds himself. Thus he will always find the diametrically opposed polarities, or opposition and constructiveness, in direct relationship to such evolutionary factors as he has conceived and placed within his mind.

In the future day when man ascends into the spiritual dimensions and has freed his mind, there will of course be the negative stance of his philosophy; or by the same token we could say that man could not ascend into this higher dimension until he has removed these obstructive ideas of negation and their intent and purpose from his daily life. Thus he has evolved, and in this evolution he has now placed himself as an individual concept of negative polarity with the Infinite (God).

God moves or oscillates from positive to negative.

In this oscillation, man will also become, in his expression outwardly to his fellow man, dimensions of negative relativity within his own concept. The circumstance of evolution, as it has been portrayed to you in the various periods of history of the earth, is a direct portrayal into the working of this cosmic intelligence and into the flight of evolution of the numerous orders of intelligence, as they are contained in different individuals.

The earth itself in its flight through evolution, is another dimensional relationship in which man, in living upon this planet, becomes somewhat of an innocent victim. He becomes subjected, not only to the influence of the time and place into which he is thus incarnated, but he also becomes somewhat the victim of large orders of the structures in the harmonic relationships of the generic forces of the Universe about him. These have been somewhat loosely termed magnetic fields. They are the direct and supporting elements of all the atomic structures in the world.

The individual thus links himself into these different dimensional expressions simply by the relationship of concept within his own mind. It is very important for the individual to know that he is a participating element in the general scheme of evolution in the Mind of God, for he thus becomes a participant in this general synthesis. Thus he will evolve into the time and place of a more direct and personal relationship with the Infinite Intelligence.

Having presented to you these more abstract concepts, you will begin to develop the idea in your mind that the philosophies of the earth, as they have been rather loosely gathered into the materialistic domain which is about you, were confined so that they involved the person *only in his immediate life* and circumstance of his time. How fallacious indeed are these interpretations; for only when the embodiment of the pure truths become the necessary structural and supporting elements of his own personal philosophy and when thoroughly interjected into his life, will man free himself from the conscious domain of the material expression.

The flight of the soul, or the evolution of man through the time and space of God's great cosmic universes is not one which is of happenstance, but one which comes through the regular organized channels of conception, as he links himself in direct relationship with the harmonic structures of God's Infinite Intelligence. It cannot be otherwise.

In his future evolution on the planet earth, it would be well if man could include in his philosophies the necessary structures whereby he could see himself as a vital and participating individual in a cosmic scheme of evolution. It would not only involve his own planet, in his own dimension and in his own time—as he calls his earth life span of three-score and ten—but he would also include in his hypothesis the necessary spiritual elements whereby he would see himself living in other worlds and in other dimensions. These worlds are infinite in number and infinite in expression; and man will relate himself to these worlds directly in proportion to the compounded elements of his own innermost nature, as he has derived them from the experience of his present terrestrial existence.

Until such time in the future, your brother,

— Kuthumi

CHAPTER 78

Hello there! For my personal identity, I was formerly known on your earth as a scientist by the name of William Crookes, and I lived in good old England somewhere in the beginning of the early 1900's. I was interested in psychic phenomenon as well as in the development of certain electronic devices. However, biographies or histories will tell you more of these things, if you so desire to read them.

As this next transmission is of a very technical nature, I contrived to be the one who was chosen to deliver these excerpts from the compositions of the different minds. As you have rightly supposed by now, the composition of truth is very technical in nature, and indeed it is so. The vast cosmic and celestial universes, in whatever dimension they exist, are in themselves compositions and expressions of energy. It will have also been resolved in your minds by this time, as was given to you by Brother Pearce in a previous transmission, that the expression of energy was related in these different dimensions as vibrations.

A very important part of this concept was purposely omitted at that time, inasmuch as we know the human mind can absorb wisdom only drop by drop; therefore, we must take the concepts step by step, so that they may further infiltrate the consciousness of the individual.

Like Brother Pearce, I cannot overemphasize the importance of the understanding of what energy is.

We have resolved there is nothing solid, for all is energy. Consequently, in our most logical conclusion or the pursuit of our hypothesis, we come to the definite conclusive fact that *God Himself is Energy,* and that he (if you want to call It, He), is the source of all energy in whatever dimensions It is expressing Itself. Therefore, it is logical to assume that if we better understand God and our relationship to Him in the different dimensions, we shall understand what energy is.

It is for this purpose that I am giving you a digest of some branches of physics, as it is called in the science of the earth; and even though you may have had some of these concepts of the physical laws included in your training or schooling, may I point out that this discussion can also be of great advantage to you, for these things will be somewhat refreshed and brought into your perspective in a different way, in order that they may be included in your concepts.

In the immediate future, you are to be taken into the second portion of Parhelion in which these very scientific principles will be shown to you in a more direct application, as they are used in the corrective therapies in the teachings and derivatives of the teachings, as they are expressed to the students who at this time are studying these relative concepts in this section of Parhelion.

Now back to energy. In your dimension, you might say that energy can be understood a little more fully if you divide it into two different kinds. We shall call the first dynamic, or energy which is moving—as sound, heat, or light. There is also that which we shall call static energy; it is really dynamic in its own dimension, but it expresses itself as atomic structures. These in turn compound the molecular structures of the 101 known elements in atomic weights, as they

718

are compounded by the earth scientist. May I put in a word of praise for the earth scientist in his work, for he has derived a good deal of truthful evaluation in the physical world about him. Now if he would just go on and get a little more of the spiritual concepts, he would indeed be a man of great value and purpose to mankind about him.

Energy, as it is in your expression or dimension, or in any other dimension for that matter, must, and always does, travel in some form. This form is called, for practical purposes, a wave. If we toss a stone into a pond, we form what is called a wave. In tossing the stone into the pond, we see energy being converted into the form of waves which travel toward the shore in a regular succession of cycles.

Energy, whether it is static or dynamic, is convertible; by that I mean that we can convert static energy into dynamic or vice versa. A practical evaluation of this fact would be, as the sun transmits energy to the earth which warms and heats it, the waters of the ocean are thereby evaporated into the cloud masses which later form rain, and eventually become the rivers on the continents of the world. These, in turn, can propel the hydroelectric power plants, generating the electricity which lights your homes. This is one conversion of dynamic energy into static and again back into dynamic form.

The trees on the mountain sides are also converted from the same sunlight. Just as in the ages past, the great coal and petroleum deposits were actually sunlight which was converted into cellulose, and compressed in great coal or peat beds in the subsurface of the earth. The nylon garments which you ladies wear at this time, are actually converted sunlight which fell upon the earth millions of years ago. So, we can see numerous examples of energy as it is converted to static forms or vice versa.

Even the process of energy conversion is going on very rapidly in your body at all times. The very fact that you are warm means that energy is being converted into heat. It is also converted into cell structures, bones and tissues, and into such plasmic structures as blood, or the spleen, or the various other constituents of the body. It is our generally shared belief that understanding the true nature of God will relate you to a proper understanding of the biological, or, shall I say, natural synthetic processes which are revolving around you in your own dimension. These convey to your mind, a great deal of the natural and latent intelligence in the expression of energy in all its dimensional factors and expressions.

To clarify the understanding of this energy, it has been pointed out in previous discussions in the book, that energy must travel in some form in what is termed a sine wave frequency. If you take a long straight piece of copper wire, or some such material, and bend it into a succession of S-formed waves, all of equal length and regular spacings, so that it forms an up-and-down wavelike motion, you will have a rough picture of what this sine wave looks like.

The energy which travels over your light wire and thereby gives you electric light, travels in some such form. You will better understand how it travels if you will walk rapidly with this coiled piece of wire held straight before you. It does not move the ethers or the etheric substances which you call space, or the dimension in which it is; instead, it moves through space in a wave form which comes from the television transmitter and is picked up by your television set. Thus your television set is synchronized or locked with the wave form which comes from the transmitter.

There is another curious thing about this energy as it is expressed as electricity. We can take this same curved piece of wire, and at regular intervals—both at top and bottom—bend into it small steps. These steps will, in consequence, be repeated time after time, in our understanding of the sine wave frequencies. In the vacuum tube of your TV set, the technician has placed a small piece of wire, just as in your light globe, through which must pass a great deal of energy which in itself, it cannot tolerate. The fact that the air has been extracted from the surrounding globe means that the wire will not be consumed although it becomes red-hot or white-hot.

The energy traveling over this wire agitates the atomic structures of the wire in what is called resistance. In other words there seems to be so much conflict going on in this wire, that it becomes red-hot or white-hot. The energy which is flowing into it is, to a large extent, casting off some of the broken up atomic structures of the wire itself. The wire will disintegrate in time to a point where it will become unfunctional, or when it can cast off no more of itself, it becomes a dead radiator.

Now if we place a small piece of metal in conjunction with this white-hot or red-hot wire, and put some positively charged electricity on the face of the plate, we shall find that the electrons, or the small energies, are attracted from the white-hot wire to the plate. If we further put a small coil of other wire between this plate and the filament, and so charge it either negatively or positively, we can modulate the transferences of energy from the filament to the plate. This principal of the vacuum tube, developed by De Forest, makes possible a great deal of energy transference in the numerous electronic devices of your world today.

Now, by adding additional resistance and capacity

in the circuitry which goes into the functioning of this vacuum tube, we can say that the energy, as it goes in, is in an "S" wave form, and that it emerges in an "S" wave form. It can be further modulated so that it can carry into itself other wave forms which can be interpreted in some other relationship as light or sound. Thus your radio can become a sound producer because, in the end result, the final vacuum tube produces energy of a sufficiently modulated nature that it is directly translated to the cone or radiating area of the speaker in the confines of the voice coil of magnetic structures.

Now I know this seems to be very highly technical in nature to you, therefore, I shall attempt to resolve it into a more simple and understandable form, so that the layman as well as the more scientifically inclined individual can evaluate what it means. Any wave form in any dimension carries within itself, its intelligence, or that which we call its superimposed wave structure.

If you could examine the instruments in the various laboratories or radio shops in your cities, you would find an instrument which is known as the oscilloscope. The technician there could couple it to your TV set so that you would actually see the picture expressed in a certain position of a very highly curved shaped wave form as it progressed through the different circuits or various parts of the TV set. The picture thus appearing would be merely a mass of tiny wiggly lines, which appeared in a certain section of this wave. To your own advantage, you might stop by the TV department in one of the stores and ask the technician to show you this particular phenomenon; it is indeed very interesting.

Upon these concepts of radiation of energy from very hotly heated filaments, I have based the construction of that which is known as the Crookes' tube. The Roentgen or the X-ray tube, is also a somewhat similar evaluation which projects intense radiation into a very high dimension of vibration.

At this time we know that vibration is the number of times, or the frequency, at which the wave will occur as its basic fundamental frequency, and we also know that the wave can carry additional frequencies, which are called its intelligence. It is these additional frequencies, which are in the formation of the wave that determines that which is superimposed within the wave itself. This same concept is carried on into the structures of the psychic body, and into the tiny vortexes, just as they are in the atomic structures. The disintegrated atoms which fly off a cathode or filament are such portions of this atomic structure which are the junctions, or parallaxes of numerous frequency integrations. They were formerly called electrons or neutrons.

If you had a microscope sufficiently powerful to look into these parallaxes, or the junction of the numerous wave forms of the atom, you would see there, a great amassment of the intelligent wave structures carried in the wave forms themselves. Extending this concept on down and down, we could re-create and re-create additional dimensions with the aid of more and more powerful microscopes, down into Infinity, or perhaps I should say on up into Infinity. (Actually, Infinity extends in all directions).

This begins to give us a rough idea of what vibration means in the higher dimensions; for we are carrying the atom upward as it should truly be carried, not downward. The vibration or currents of the pulsations or frequencies of energy structures will determine, to a large extent, in what dimension it expresses itself. But the main point to remember is that all energy does express a certain intelligence, and that it re-creates and re-creates this intelligence as long as it is permitted to express itself without being changed, or, shall I say, rectified or re-impinged by future consequences of other energy forms which exist as harmonic transients.

As was explained by the simple allegory of the piano keyboard, energy is sympathetic to itself, according to the occurrence, or rate of vibration of any other similarly vibrating structure. Thus we generate harmonics, or what is called superharmonics or subharmonics, occurring at a direct multiple of two and one-half times the original two basic fundamental frequencies. This, in your dimension, is called the law of harmonic frequency relationship. Even your radios are attuned to function in this dimensional capacity. These same mathematical formulae can be carried up into other equivalents into other dimensions. We can thus begin to evaluate the importance of having a knowledge of the meaning of energy. We must properly constitute our concept into a form which will enable us to picture what the dimension is in which we are existing. Such wisdom will give you an insight into how God really works in the dimension with which you are associated at the present time.

Many of you who will read these lines, have not, in the past, taken a great deal of interest in what is called physics or the various biological processes, whether they are in the dimension of the animal or vegetable kingdoms. I would like to point out also, that in the sine wave, you will be able to see that a large curved line may contain many little wiggly lines, and as they are wiggling around the larger line, will convey to you something of that which we call a superimposed frequency vibration.

Just take a piece of paper and draw an elongated "S" on it, just as you have been previously instructed to do in other transmissions. You will see that if you put a plus sign at the top and a minus sign at the bottom, you have formed a basic sine wave. Now you can draw some other little lines which are going around and around and within a certain portion of the top and a certain portion of the bottom of this "S".

This will give you a somewhat crude picture of how the actual transmission of the picture from the TV station into your TV set would look, if you could see it on the oscilloscope. On the other side of this "S" you will also see a little jerky place, or a step. This is what is called a sinc pulse or it is a vibration, or frequency, of 60 times a second, which is superimposed on this original large "S" or basic sine wave. This locks in the picture properly as it occurs and recurs through the transmitter, so that you see the picture as it is properly transmitted from the broadcasting station.

I am drawing this allegory for you and re-emphasizing it for the simple reason that it is directly the same process by which you evolve in the various evolutions on your earth, as you are actually living from day to day and from moment to moment. The little television pictures are projected into your consciousness, or other structures of your psychic body, with each experience of an emotional nature in which you have lived at some previous time. I do not necessarily mean this life in which you are now living. These wave forms in your psychic body could have existed there for many hundreds, or even thousands of years, depending on their nature, their frequency, and their intensity; also depending on whether you have cancelled them out by the proper application of the specified form of spiritual therapy, which we shall call, for the moment, psychotherapy. Literally then, you are—in a pure sense of the word—a walking TV station.

We can also carry this concept a little further and involve the Superconscious Mind and all of the other dimensions around you; for in the relationship translations of these energy wave forms into your psychic body and, consequently, into your mind, you can thus see how you may become clairvoyant, as it is called. This is the basic concept for psychic phenomenon; in a more crude and elemental form, it is called spiritualism; but, there is a great deal more than spiritualism in Psychic Science. Psychic science, in a pure scientific aspect, should be a science or a philosophy of life which would properly integrate these concepts into every way in which you live in every moment of your life, and should not be confined to the seance room, where a few discarnate entities could come to you and give you a little sympathy or understanding in the knowledge that they are still living.

Your science or understanding of psychic phenomenon thus includes a factual, integrated and workable concept, which includes something just beyond that which we shall call the intuitional boundary. You will actually see around you, with the understanding and inclusion of the knowledge of such dimensional factors, which relate you to the higher dimensions of concepts. For as you gain this understanding that the higher forces are working in harmony, and in conjunction with you, as you will allow them, by integrating these concepts into your philosophy of life, thus the inclusion of your application and understanding of these things will manifest itself into the world about you.

You will begin to see a great deal more of law, order, and harmony in everything you do. You will not be forced, as a consequence of the great amount of negativity which is around you, to include this negativity in your own relationship of life. You will not easily yield to negative energies—viruses, colds or other body disturbances which may come to you—for you may then be protected against incurring such bodily discomforts.

Other factors which enter into your understanding of this frequency relationship and the dimensional factors about you, will also manifest themselves to your friends and relatives. You will come into harmonic conclusion with everything around you in life, to which you are directed, and in whatever you are included.

Referring again to the concept of tossing the stone into the pond, the energy which you have transferred by means of moving the stone in an arc with your arm, forms a trajectory into a regular arc, as the stone falls into the water. This energy is absorbed into the water as a wave form; or the water absorbs and manifests it as a wave form. You will also notice a curious phenomenon; the farther away the waves get from the original disturbance where the stone entered the water, the farther and farther apart the waves will be and, as a consequence, they are larger and larger and seem to move slower and slower.

In a similar manner in your own dimension, the farther you get into the terrestrial or physical dimensions, you will find that all the spectrums of energy, as they are expressed in your world, will have a vibrating frequency, or a recurrence, or a pulse of a corresponding largeness, which will cause them to occur and recur at longer and longer intervals.

You were told that in the higher dimensions, frequencies occurred which were beyond the concepts of your finite mind, and this is true. The process called vibrotherapy, which is produced by the use of crystals in the present day world of the hospitals, frequencies are produced up to one million times per second. I would say that the frequency recurrence is as slow as a snail, compared with your jet airplane, in comparison to the frequency rate in some of the higher dimensions. Yes, I could use even a much greater difference of comparison, if it could be so postulated in your mind.

In your everyday life—as has been previously explained—in different things about you, you will see a great deal of this energy transference; for, as the energy remanifests in countless and numerous ways, it becomes either dynamic or static. The energy coming from the sun is transferred into frequency spectrums which are known as light and heat. Light coming into your eyes falls through the lens into the retina or the back portion of the eye, which is composed of large masses of cones and rods. On the apexes of these cones and rods are small cells which are composed of organic chemicals such as phosphorus.

Light waves strike these cells; and because light waves are unsuitable to be transferred directly into the brain, they must be, shall I say, converted into a different frequency before they can be acceptable to your brain. Therefore, in the process of the light falling onto these chemicals, there is a certain photosynthesis, or transference of energy, which will again relate the energy of light into a frequency which is acceptable to your brain as a form of consciousness.

The pictures of light which the eyes are capable of transferring to the brain occur at a certain cycle or frequency, of about twenty pictures per second. Consequently, you cannot take any more pictures in, nor can you exclude any pictures except by closing the lids of your eyes. The pictures occur and recur at a certain basic rate of twenty times per second, the process being involved, as I have just explained, is through the degeneration of various chemicals which are contained in the cells of the rods and cones in the retina of the eye.

The same process is again used in your television set, in that the screen, or the large part of the tube in front of you, is coated with the same kind of phosphoric compounds as are found in the rods and cones of the eyes. They retain, for a certain split fraction of a second, the tiny impressions of light waves; or, expressed more correctly, they are in the electronic beam as it comes from the cathode at the rear of the tube. The spot, as it is called, moves across the face of the tube at the rate of about sixteen thousand times per second, and like a line, it writes back and forth across the face of the tube. The phosphorus on the face of the tube momentarily holds each receding spot as it moves back and forth across the screen, thus forming a complete picture for your eye, since the eye is unable to distinguish that there has been a succession of many spots across the face of the tube. This is something of an optical illusion.

A similar process is used in the motion picture theater, as the image is projected on the screen. However, I shall not digress too far or go into other fields of expression, so as not to confuse you too much, since this transmission was primarily intended to convey to you what it means to evaluate energy properly as it is used in an integrated order of concept in your daily lives.

In the future explorations into the center of Parhelion which is just before you, you shall be taken to witness psychotherapy being taught and explained to the various students. Principles of such a nature require your understanding as to how energy exists in different dimensions and how it manifests and remanifests itself according to its wave form or frequency (IQ), or that it is composed and recomposed of superimposed frequencies within itself (regeneration).

Again I would like to compliment the earth scientist and the individual who has pursued the course of the physical sciences into somewhat of a metaphysical dimension; for his perseverance has resulted in the vast amount of progress which has been made manifest in approximately the past fifty years. The metaphysical inclusion is just as important for the future, because his science will reach a stalemate, or a form of degeneration if he does not include these dimensional relationships within it. Also it has been pointed out repeatedly in previous transmissions, that these concepts are vitally necessary for the evolution of the people in their progress on the earth today. In fact, the salvation of all mankind is determined by the direct proportions of these dimensional or spiritual concepts which are included in the future lives and evolutions of man on the earth.

Since the earth itself is evolving into a spiritual cosmic state of consciousness, man, by necessity, must be in tune or in harmony with the Infinite Mind of God in the overall evolution of the terrestrial earth. He must not just merely tag along like a small doggie beside his master; instead, he himself must become a master. He must begin to understand what is meant by being clairvoyant. Brother Pearce very firmly emphasized the necessity of the inclusion of these concepts in the field of psychiatry, psychology, and medicine. Likewise, I firmly emphasize that they must also be included in the physical sciences as they are expressed in the world today; for we regret there is indeed a great preponderance of physical science which is not conclusively proved, or which does not include such spiritual concepts; consequently it loses much of its value or usefulness to mankind in general.

If it were possible for the average spiritualist medium on the earth today to be trained in the basic elements of electronics or physical sciences, that person would become a much more useful organ of expression to mankind in general. In like manner, the physicist and the chemist on the earth today, in proportion to their knowledge of spiritual structures and the transmissions of energy in its expression in higher dimensions, would be able to do as they do in the other worlds which are about you. You could build your space ships, eliminate all your diseases and solve the various problems of mankind as they exist with you today. You could—as they do in other worlds —eliminate almost to one hundred per cent, the various mental aberrations which are now existent on your planet earth.

At a future time, a great deal more of this knowledge will be given to you in a less scientific concept, one which will relate largely to the governmental aspects of the nation of America, and to the world in general. Now, unless there are any further questions which may arise in the moments which follow, I shall close and remain your brother in spirit.

— Crookes

CHAPTER 79

Hello again! I believe it is a privilege, which has been exercised several times in the past, to add a P.S. to the previous transcript, and although many of the scientists and physicists of the earth and other worlds are here with me, I have bowed gracefully to the need to return and will gratefully give you something more of the remaining part or parts of my previous transmission. As you have rightfully guessed, this is Crookes again.

With me here are Newton, Voltaire, Spencer and I could name quite a few others who are very anxious that the correct evaluation and interpretation be given into the constituents of a universal concept. The precepts of this concept will determine to a large degree how much constructive philosophy you will obtain from the pages of this book.

The whole nature of understanding about the higher dimensions will involve processes of thinking which you might consider at your time and in your place as being very technical and quite involved. However, in their proper dimension and in their proper order, they will be much more easily understood and assimilated. But it was upon the theory, that an ounce of prevention is worth a pound of cure, that we believe an ounce of preparation will prevent many future reincarnations, by making you a person who can more suitably and more quickly evolve into a state of consciousness which will be more compatible with your original nature. Let us pause for a moment and review what we have learned.

In the opening transcripts of the book, great emphasis was placed on concept. This was necessary to tear you loose, as it has been termed, from the very adhesive thought patterns which you had incurred through the reincarnations of earth life. As we progressed farther along in the book, newer and newer concepts were brought into focus and enlarged upon, to a degree which could more readily be absorbed by the layman or truth seeker.

Thus it was that the whole context of the philosophy resolved itself into the fact that because there were an innumerable and infinite number of dimensions of expression, and that because God is so Infinite in His nature, He expresses Himself in all these dimensions and in all possible and conceivable forms and relationships. Therefore God could *NOT* possibly be a human manifestation as is frequently pictured in the minds of many earth individuals. Thus God had to become and assume His rightful place in your consciousness as the great *Emanating and Radiating Source and Power of Intelligence* in all infinite dimensions which He has brought into your consciousness. It also further developed that since God is the universal source of energy in all manifestations, there must therefore, by necessity, be a great deal of wisdom and intelligence connected with the expression of this infinite and abstract concept.

So it is resolved that energy must and does exist in different dimensional forms. For this purpose we pointed out the various chord structures in the diatonic or chromatic scale of the piano or other instruments. These chord structures were further enlarged to the point where the piano keyboard becomes something of a dimension.

A dimension is strictly a place in which there are certain lines of demarcation, or shall we say, certain barriers have been circumscribed around the functioning of the various energy spectrums within this dimension, just as there are in your life upon this planet earth, and thus you see in the ultimate expression of energy, the speed of light. This circumscribes the absolute concept of the movement of the dynamic form of energy into its next or more relevant plane of expression.

Between the speed of light and that which is called mass, are many other spectrums of such relationships of dynamic or static energy. These have been explained to you as merely movements of dynamic or static force, and in the ultimate conclusion, all of these forces were in themselves, energy forms in such dimensional expressions. The free moving energy, as in the flash of lightning, or electricity, contrasted with the supposedly solid structures of mass which are in the world about you, is actually constituted of small microscopic worlds of energy that are expressing themselves in a direct relationship to another dimension.

It was in this latter concept that many of the scientists of the world, including myself, became rather enmeshed and embroiled at different times in our earth life. I might say that Isaac Newton became thus involved in trying to explain, to some degree, the expression of mass and energy in mathematical formulas or calculus. The banner was later taken up by such men as Max Planck, who learned that energy did not—as was supposed—express itself outwardly like water flowing through something; but that there was somewhat of a frequency or harmonic relationship of energy from one form into another. As we have learned, energy, whether molecular or atomic, expresses itself either dynamically or statically, and is inter-changeable in these forms in its true and natural sequence of evolution about you. Max Planck form-ulated his theory called "Planck's Quantum Theory," whereby he arrived at some sort of a mathematical formula for the transference of energy from one form into another.

Einstein later took the values of this calculus and further developed them into the "Theory of Relativity." Later on, in the last years of his life, he was busily engaged in formulating a new theory, which so ex-panded his original concepts that he, too, flounder-ed in the web of intricate forms of calculus which he, in his finite mind, could not grasp. The failure was very obvious for the reason that he had not related his formulas in other dimensional factors, or in that which we would term the spiritual concepts. If he had done so, he would have been in a better position—at least in his own mind—to have conceived something more of the values of his calculus. I might say, inci-dentally, that Einstein is now expressing himself in one of these higher Shamballas and is busily engaged in tearing down some of the fabrications of his mater-ial life on the earth, and replacing this superstructure of materialism with more of the abstract and infinite concepts which are clearer and more visible when one arrives in these dimensions.

It must not be inferred that I am underrating or making derogatory remarks about any of those minds who lived and served mankind in some new or ad-vanced theory or concept. We cannot underestimate the value of Archimedes in postulating the theory of his hydraulics and hydrostatics, or his theory of spe-cific gravity. Such hydraulics and hydrostatics are in use in the different interpretations of science, in ship-building and various fields in the world today. Likewise, all of these philosophies or sciences, as they have been expressed on the earth at one time or another, contain certain elements of truth which are immortal and imperishable. The concepts may have been contradictory or interwoven with materialistic aspects; or they may have been so confined that they did not include certain spiritual concepts which rendered their value somewhat less than they normally would have been, had they included the spiritual or higher dimensional factors of relationships. However, these things must be rendered to mankind, each in its time and in its proper sequence, otherwise it is of little value to mankind.

Very often the concepts which are expounded into the world are very much in advance of their time, as will be substantiated by Alexander Graham Bell, who tried vainly to sell people the idea that he could talk over a wire. I might also point out that Samuel B. Morse, with whom I am acquainted, almost starved to death in his attic before he could convince a few notables of that time, to come to him that he might send the message from one room to another: "What hath God wrought?"

There must always be leaders in all fields, as these things are, in themselves, all the values or relative equations which are or are not acceptable to the general trend of philosophies, or the levels of mentality, as are expressed in a general way with mankind as he exists at this time and at this place. There must always be the way-showers, and frequently at the expense of their own reputations, and in some instances even at the sacrifice of their lives, in order to show man a newer and better way to arrive at some basic concepts of life.

Pursuing our course in the understanding of energy, we were somewhat reviewing our sequence of transmissions and summing up to a point of foci, whereby we could be a little more conclusive—for the time being—so that you might be led into the different dimensions here in the second section of Parhelion. The principles of energy relationship of these higher orders could actually be demonstrated to you for the benefit of those who read these lines as they are written in this book, and so we have laid such strong emphasis on the individual, whether layman or the more advanced scientifically minded person in his own dimension of concept.

The study of the atoms, which number from one to one hundred according to their atomic weights, is, in itself, one of great value as it relates to the different ways in which it is expressed into your material life, as you have called these atomic structures, or masses of atoms of solid substance. This study is also one which is very fascinating, since it relates as it does to your own New Age, or as you call it, the Atomic Age.

It has been repeatedly pointed out that the scientists of this day and time know very little, if anything, about the atom. This statement seems to be a rather broad one, which is liable to arouse a great deal of antagonism. However, we are fully justified in making this assertion; furthermore we can prove that which we say is true. It has not been so long since the scientists believed the atom to be composed of solid particles. The scientists in nuclear physics today, are generally conceding the fact that there are no solid fractions or portions in an atom, and even the nucleus itself seems to be dissolving into masses of energy. As we have explained before so very carefully, the relationship of the atom depends entirely upon its relationship to a higher dimension.

It is the constant extending of the energy from this higher dimension into each atom, which makes it a positive potential of energy and thus relates it in a negative fashion to the material world. In atomic or nuclear physics the scientists of your time have merely succeeded in disrupting or blowing apart these wave forms; and the energy which the scientists thought was contained in the atom, was not contained in it at all. A little better picture of the situation can be given by saying that the uranium of the U-235, or similar quotient, which is fissionable material, has existed in the earth's structures, as an element, for something like two billion years, using the figures of your own dimension of time. This atom which has existed in your earth dimension and in your quotient of time for two billion years, has expended into your dimension in its form of molecular adhesion, as you call the structures of elements, the quotient of energy which is capable of expressing as two billion years. However, the dimension in which this energy was thus expressed into the atom was not confined by the principle of time. In other words, the next two billion years—as far as this dimension was concerned—could very easily have been expressed in a matter of two seconds, or even two fractions of a second.

The earth scientist, in triggering this atom and blowing it apart, has merely realized the utmost impact of the existence of the atom in your dimension, in the terms of power or energy of the life of two billion years of that atom, as it has been expressed from its higher dimension of relationship. A rather crude allegory would be something which would lead up to a more understandable situation. We would say, for example, (as I have previously placed the equation in the mind of the Channel), a man is blowing up a toy balloon from a tank of gas and somewhere in the process, the balloon bursts and the gas escaped into the air. Before the man can grab the valve and shut off the gas from the tank, some of the gas has rushed forth from the tank and into the air. This is rather crude, inasmuch as the actual exploding of the atom itself merely releases into your third dimension, the equivalent of the entire lifetime of that atom as it exists on your earth plane; simply because the concept of time is not expressed in the third dimensional equation of its existence in the dimension from whence it sprang. In other words, it has existed not only in its own true dimension or spiritual relationship as a pure or a higher form of energy for two billion years, but for an infinite length of time; and it expressed only a certain cycle of relationship in a lower dimension in the factor of the element of time. This it did with the elements of wave forms and vortexes as they have been previously described to you.

This was a rather abstract understanding that related the expression of energy to the higher concept which involved the pure, and more infinite nature of God's intelligent energy. The atom thus contained a multitude of these expressions of Infinite energy which could have been directed either destructively or constructively. Only in the last few years of the earth scientist's expression in nuclear energy, has man been able to infuse certain principles of radionics into atomic structures, such as cobalt and iodine, and to render these elements, or the compositions of these elements, into what has been termed isotopes or radioactive agencies, whereby they can be used in the treatment of various maligned conditions in the human body, such as cancer or hypothyroidism, and in various other ways in which the doctors and the men of medicine are learning to use this newer concept of energy.

In the future it may be that man on the earth will learn to tap the atom just as he would insert a spigot into the end of a barrel to withdraw the wine or the beer. However, such a concept is not immediately in prospect, for the scientists have merely devised this science as a means of defense or offense, in the undertaking of war as it is propagated among the races of mankind. The association of time in the element of energy transference in the third dimension, in which the earth exists, has always been one which has somewhat confounded the various savants as they have tried to gain a more intelligent relationship with the creative forces which they vaguely knew were extending, not only within themselves, but were also manifesting in the innumerable and infinite aspects of nature about them.

These inward longings and relationships to man's inward and outward expression, as he calls God, have caused him to pursue this course of philosophy or science or some such inspirational outlet in his own personal nature. However, these evolutions of man and his thinking are, by necessity, products of the relationship of the dimension in which the earth is progressing at its particular time. You have seen how energy relates itself in the natural order of sequence or harmonics and that each dimension is linked to another. Furthermore, within each dimension is contained the chord structures, or spectrums, necessary for this natural order of harmonic relationship which exists, not only throughout the terrestrial planets and the terrestrial universes, but also up into the cosmos of celestial expression, which is sometimes very erroneously called time and space.

If the scientist on the earth today could gain one small peek or glimpse beyond the level of the finite or material world in which he exists, and become clairvoyant—he would, just as have you, become so staggered that he would be mentally confused in trying to bring even a small portion of this great relative, expansive universe within the confined dimension of his own finite mind.

We have tried, in our theoretical concepts, to bring to your consciousness, the fact that you are similar to a walking, living television set. Your daily expressions are merely the reflections onto the outward screen of your life as you express it in your daily life from time to time, as you call the present. These reflections are then compounded and reflected onto this screen from the emotional experiences of your past lives. By the same process you can relate yourself to the higher dimensions whereby you can begin to express, shall I say, in an inspirational way, the higher concepts which are related to the dimensions in which the true nature of God exists, in a much more realistic fashion than it does in the material world or dimension in which you are now living.

We would say that if the average individual who lives on the earth today, steeped as he is in the traditions, lusts, and desires of the material world; so concerned with his beer, his cigarettes, and his sex; his eating and sleeping and the money he makes, could momentarily peer just beyond his immediate grasp of mind, he, too, might likewise be so shocked and confounded that he would never be the same person again. He might be knocked entirely off the center of his equilibrium and become somewhat unbalanced.

It is therefore natural in the sequence of evolution of each individual that he must arrive basically and within the domain of his own consciousness, to exercise this franchise in order that he may constructively proceed along the lines of evolution into the higher dimensions; otherwise he will surely destroy himself.

We have tried, from time to time, to explain to you

741

that the various sections of Shamballa were, within themselves, so sectionalized that the individual could thus become attuned to a more and more compatible rate of vibration, as it has been called, and in some ways into his own natural line of thought; or, perhaps you might term it, into his own ray.

In the concepts of astrology, many people try to confine this dimension of energy and frequency transference into the realm of pure and somewhat elemental astrophysics, or as it relates to energy transference from magnetic structures of other planets. If the astrologer would thoroughly and conscientiously pursue a scientific line of investigation for the next few hundred years, he could properly relate the concepts of his mind so that he would more thoroughly integrate a true basic concept of astrology. He would then understand how man was, and is, constantly reflecting into his own consciousness, the proper relationship and perspective of the different dimensions of energy which are more or less immediately associated with his daily life.

The small and rather fractional values of magnetic influence, as they are concerned by the revolutions of the planets in their orbits, are in themselves, slightly more than nothing; for, as has been commonly stated, the planets impel but do not compel. The mere action or belief which arises from the action or belief in itself, of such a concept, will give more credence, will give more power to this concept, and in such beliefs, you may be led further and further astray from the path of Truth.

Do not at any time, attempt to confine the extractions of your mentality into such channels as shall be defined by any one or even several concepts; instead, become universal in your nature. Reach out with the power or the Superconsciousness which is within you, and as you progress, relate and draw into you, such fractions or particles of these dimensional factors of relationship, so that you impound and include these into the sequence of evolution of your being. Thus you shall truly become Godlike in your nature; and thus you shall become of greater value and service to your fellow man.

Until a further time, we await your pleasure.

— Crookes, Newton, Spencer, and Others.

CHAPTER 80

Greetings to my brothers and sisters on the earth!

This is the individual identified as Alessandro Volta, an Italian, who lived on the earth about the time of Benjamin Franklin. Your history will relate me to the field of electronics and science in which I had something to do with putting together a battery. As a result, my name Volta was changed to "volt," as a denotation of electronic energy or pressure.

I am sorry if I disappoint you, because I am not Voltaire. (Ruth expressed a mental note of surprise as she thought Voltaire was to be guide. He noted it and stated that it could be arranged should we desire such contact.) As you see, our names are quite similar. However, Voltaire is available in this vicinity and would be most happy to render any service which he is capable of giving.

We are hoping you will all be very patient with us here in our somewhat rather lengthy discussion of the atom, for it must be remembered that although you may not be able to assimilate all of the information which we can give you at this time, yet it is most vital and necessary for the future generations of mankind. Although we believe you may not understand thoroughly at the present time, yet at some future day you will quite likely be able to absorb the full content of this information.

Now, getting back to the atom, for we would not

leave you halfway in the middle of the stream and you are still somewhat puzzled by the fact that an atom can liberate so much energy into the world in what is called an atomic explosion. I shall begin by saying that an atom, in a way, can be similarized to a human being. An atom is intelligent; it has a definite period of evolution, of incarnation, and of reincarnation. An atom also radiates and absorbs energy, and does many things which are peculiar to atoms alone. So let us examine these qualities of atoms individually, that we may best learn of their true nature.

In the scale of atomic weights, as given by the scientists of your time, we shall begin with hydrogen and go up, as we shall say, into the heavier, or, as is sometimes termed, the fissionable materials of uranium. The hydrogen atom is a comparatively simple or an elementarily developed atom, inasmuch as to the earth scientist it merely involves a nucleus and a supposed electron or a positron revolving in an orbit around it. A more true concept of this simple atom means that it is merely connected to a certain dimension through the orbit of energy as it is expressed in the electron which is revolving around it; thus this electron in itself, is simply the apex or the core nucleus of the dimension or vortex to which it is attached.

Now in the pattern or life cycle of atoms, they must evolve in some such similar fashion as a human being, or a plant, or an animal. God's Infinite Intelligence is here expressed in the same relative concepts in which it is expressed in other dimensions and lines of energy expression.

The difference here is that when we call an atom intelligent, we do not mean the same kind of intelligence which a man or a beast may have. In mankind, intelligence is strictly based on, or is a product of his emotional experience, as it evolves around him during his lifetime or in his many lifetimes. In the case of the atom, the intelligence comes, not only from within itself, as it is linked to this dimension or vortex in a spiritual way, but it gains more intelligence by the association of other elemental structures of atoms around it and thus it is in no way emotional. It is merely the functioning of certain relative laws of harmonic structures. Consequently in the future, if the hydrogen atom is not destroyed by some silly experiment, it—and I am speaking of the hydrogen atom—will gradually resolve back into its spiritual dimension and will recur on some terrestrial or material planet as a more highly developed atom. It will continually take into itself the necessary vortexes, or the expressions of other supporting energy sources from the higher dimensions around it; so that it becomes more and more complex in nature. Thus it arrives at a comparatively high rate of expression of structure as an uranium atom.

It is on the basis of this understanding that the earth scientist has said that the uranium atom has existed for two billion years. Actually, if he could see into the spiritual dimensions where time was non-existent in the sense that it is in your world, he would see that that atom existed and expressed energy in the quotient or equivalent of earth time to a much larger degree. It might truly be said that the atom was a hundred billion years old.

Now the atom has other peculiar qualities. It will radiate energy. This is done in a number of ways. As you all know, certain metals have a definite odor; so do other chemicals which are called elements, and the substances which are compounded into these elements all exhibit their odors. We do not necessarily confine or evaluate the properties of such volatile liquids, as are contained in perfume, or such kindred substances wherein the atomic structures are kept in a comparatively high state of agitation, because their natural density depends on the temperature or the thermonuclear expansion within the sometimes so-called molecular structure.

An earth physicist or scientist knows that an atom radiates. This is proven by the mere fact that if he wishes to combine two atoms, he finds a great deal of difficulty, unless he places within the immediate proximity, a third element or an atomic structure. The first two original atoms will then combine very readily and without involving the third atomic structure. This is called the principle of catalysis, meaning that the third element has thus become a catalyst. Now, in the properties of radiation, the atom or a group of atoms all can be said to be radiating simultaneously in a certain harmonic structure, quite similar to what is produced on the piano keyboard.

If we examine a bar of steel, we can understand what is meant by strong radiation factors in some of the more highly developed atoms. A bar of steel is said to be hard. It is hard simply because of the rate of vibration within the atoms themselves as they manifest this vibration outwardly (from themselves) in certain chord structures, whereby they link and re-link themselves in a certain manner by very definite strong lines of force which we shall call for want of a better name, magnetic forces.

Now, a bar of metal—such as steel—if brought into the proximity of a very highly charged magnetic field of alternating current, will immediately become magnetized. This can be done because the intelligence of atoms, as expressed in a certain dispensation in the law of general harmonic relations into molecular structures, is now realigned into a very definite radiating expression; so from both ends of this bar of steel we shall see two polarities of very strong magnetic force.

Nothing has been visibly changed within the structure of the steel itself. It merely means that instead of the atoms expressing themselves in a general outward way, they are now linking themselves together in a certain harmonic chord structure towards both ends of the steel bar. These properties of permanent magnetism in steel can be further enhanced and strengthened to a remarkable degree, as the earth scientists have found, by the inclusion of a small amount of nickel. Nickel is a nonferrous metal and is nonmagnetic, but the inclusion of two or three percent of this bright and silvery metal in the bar of steel, will further catalyze the expression of radiating qualities of the atoms of the steel itself; so that they not only become aligned to a much greater degree of strength, but they also retain that alignment for a much greater period of time. Thus you have developed some strong magnetic structures.

At the present time on earth, the science of chemistry is very highly developed. The earth chemist of today is able to combine molecular structures of different atoms in such a manner that he is able to produce hundreds of thousands of synthetic drugs, dyes, and plastics; due to the differences in molecular composition whereby certain groups of atomic structures are so diametrically opposed to each other, that they may take on and present to each other entirely different properties of intelligence. The fact that an atom is an atom of such and such a substance, is determined entirely by what that atom is radiating into the outward or the material world around us, an inviolate fact known to be true of the very compositions of two atomic substances found all over the earth and acknowledged by any earth scientist. It is found very freely in the waters of the ocean, yet any chemist or scientist knows how extremely difficult it is to separate the salt because it is composed of a gas called chlorine and an element, or a metallic mineral called sodium, simply because the atomic structures of the two elements are merged or interlocked in their composition in the manner in which they radiate in their own vortexes. Any such dissociation or combination of atomic structures in their changing, or in their potentialities, is extremely difficult in the present knowledge of the earth scientists.

During the Middle Ages, a great deal of emphasis was brought into the focus of public attention by what was called the philosopher's stone. By the mysterious properties of catalysis, the philosopher believed he would develop some sort of a composition of elements, whereby he could touch some other basic element, such as lead, and transmute it into gold. The problem of transmutation, or changing elements from one to another, as it exists in your present day, is an extremely involved and complicated process and one which involves an expenditure of a great deal of time and money, and, as a consequence, it is of little or no value to the general purpose of life about you.

This is indeed fortunate, otherwise you would see a large number of scientists going about manufacturing gold which would plunge the financial world of your day into complete chaos. It would also, in the blindness of expression in man's being and his unintelligent way of expressing life toward himself, completely throw the balance of the basic structures of elements out of gear; and he would probably end up with a planet which was composed of two or three elements, rather than one which was basically balanced and in harmonic conclusion with one hundred elements.

Man has always been in a very good position to watch the intelligent forces of nature, or God. Thus he should not attempt to divert these forces into some superimposed structure of false values about him. In his panic of fear and insecurity, as he lacks the common ingredients of spiritual knowledge, man is seeking in some manner to placate these fears within himself. If he could resolve these fears into an intelligent thought pattern, whereby he could see the continuity and the purpose of his life—individually and collectively—as it is contained in all of the elemental substances and in the various biological structures of the earth about him, he would lose this semblance of fear of death. Instead, death to him would then become a glorious conclusion of the natural functioning of certain orders or "laws" as they are expressed in God's Infinite Mind.

Man is born into the world primarily, we shall say, as two complete or opposite polarities, the material and the spiritual. He is taught from birth to become a creature of reactionary stance. He is continually fearful of concluding his life in some premature manner; thus the fear of death becomes something which causes him to do many strange things. He believes that by his collection of material values of the world, he has gained some sense of security. He believes in many different and fallacious interpretations of life which will leave him without a stable, substantiating support, and will retard his progression into his more natural conclusive state of reincarnation and evolution.

But getting back to the atoms. The earth scientist knows that atomic explosions are of two different natures: that which is called the atomic, or fissionable explosion, and that which is called the thermonuclear, or the hydrogen explosion. We have discussed somewhat the explosion of the fissionable materials, such as uranium in which the scientist, in blowing apart the small content of energy which is contained in this uranium atom, is actually liberating the whole akashic body or the spiritual counterpart of this atom, as it is poised somewhere halfway between your dimension and the spiritual dimension of its origin. He thus liberates into the material world, a vast amount of energy, which would otherwise be unavailble to him, simply because he has instantaneously concluded, in the fraction of a split second, the entire lifetime of that atom as it was impounded in the psychic structures of that atom's superconciousness, if we can draw an allegorical equation to that of the psychic structures in a human being.

The same conditions exist in the life of the atom and in that of man in somewhat of a different form, but they exist there, nevertheless. A moment's thought on the subject and you will see the comparison in the man blowing up the toy balloon from the huge reserve of gas. A very small fractional portion of the energy released, was actually contained in the nucleus or in the atom itself; but almost the entire force came from within the spiritual realm of the atom. This in its true sense, was an outward explosion in the material world, which was called an atom bomb explosion.

The hydrogen bomb is a somewhat different situation. It realizes the release of energy from influx or implosion; that is, the collapse of two dimensions upon each other. The scientist has succeeded in taking a form of hydrogen, called heavy water, which has within its atomic structure, two so diametrically opposed dimensions or vortexes of energy, that in triggering them they fall in, or upon each other. Thus is released outwardly into the world, by the collapse of these two small dimensions, a great deal of energy; and I say a great deal, comparatively speaking, of what would be available in the simple hydrogen atoms themselves.

Here again is a much more dangerous condition than was formerly expressed in the explosion, because the scientist has now almost directly linked his experiment up to all of the basic structures of the hundred elements as they compose his terrestrial dimension. If he is not very careful in his future experiments, with the collapsing of these small psychic dimensions within each other, he will very likely wind up by triggering his whole little world into a cloud of cosmic dust.

I must very strongly emphasize this danger to the scientist of the earth. He has escaped with two or three of these thermonuclear implosions; but he may not be quite so successful if he develops them beyond the point at which he has now arrived. I can with the others, again emphasize to the strongest degree, the warning which is voiced, not only from here, but from many of the earth scientists, such as Oppenheimer, who are openly voicing the tremendous dangers of this type of explosion. It could easily affect not only your own little world and blow it into atomic dust, but could trigger as well great astral dimensions, which are immediately connected to this dimension. You might actually succeed in destroying a large part of God's terrestrial universe. *So do be careful,* my fellow scientists.

As an old timer who has lived on your earth at one time, I must re-emphasize to the utmost degree, the measures of extreme caution which you must use as you proceed along the lines of experimentation which you have developed. In the future, learn to look upon the atom as something of a more constructive evaluation. With these atomic structures you will be able to release into your dimension, vast power which is not necessarily destructive in the nature of the atomic structures from whence the power comes. In other words, you will have succeeded in arriving at a place where you will have tapped one of the sources of energy from the vast universe about you. There are a number of sources of this energy just beyond the horizon of your present-day understanding.

The people on other planets, who have arrived at some of the conclusions and understandings of the release of this vast amount of cosmic energy, have been enabled to build the space craft which you have seen as flying saucers. It has enabled them, too, to set aside diseases of various types, mental and physical derelictions, and prostitution as you see it so strongly emphasized in your world about you today.

Even the people on Mars have a much more highly advanced science than you do. They are actually able to correct any small deficiency in the psychic body of a newly born child, before he grows to an age where these retrograde expressions attain a more advanced form. These deficiencies are very quickly rectified by a certain type of electronic equipment which actually alters, from the physical side of his nature, the spiritual vortexes in the psychic body, to the extent where he grows up to be a very useful citizen, instead of becoming a criminal, or a person with perverted instincts in some manner or form.

The fear of death itself arises from the numerous facets of life on your planet, such as starvation or hunger, which might be impinged into the consciousness of the child, between his nipple-nursing and his feeding. This fear of starvation and death causes him to do many very strange things.

His predominating desire for procreation and sex also creates some very strange manifestations in his nature. The exploitation of mankind is a very highly developed technical science of the earth today among the industrialists and leaders in the financial world, who make their living by exploiting the carnal desires of man's nature. Man is continually autosuggestively motivated by the expressions in the field of advertising, whereby he becomes a victim, not only of the exploitation, but also in his attempt to arrive at certain compromises in the natural expression and the evolution of his consciousness; and by incurring these different compromises into his mind, he becomes quite neurotic and inhibited.

Any psychiatrist can tell you of at least two or three hundred different types of phobias of which the average individual is likely to have anywhere from one to a dozen or more. These are merely inhibited reflexes which stem, or arise, from some fear or as a consequence of an emotional experience in a person's life. However, this subject is psychiatry, and I shall leave it to someone who is much more worthy of dealing with these facets of life on your earth than am I. I have merely come further to conclude the knowledge of atomic structures as they are expressed into your world as definite creative potentials or expressions of God's own Infinite Mind. They should be treated thusly.

In exploding the atoms, you are actually destroying the continuity of God's purpose. So let us remember in the future, what atomic structures are, my friends and brothers and sisters. Then you will see in the expressions of life about you that these submicroscopic particles are manifestations of energy, and although they appear in your world as mass, they are all basically evolving and developing along preordained and preconceived lines in the intelligent nature of God's Mind. They are there for the purpose of making life and your present status of reincarnation possible; therefore you must learn to use all of the values of life about you constructively.

If you continue into another world war, then we can surely say that your earth will be destroyed and destroyed completely. Thus it is that we are so concerned at the present moment. It would effect not only you, but would effect us and many hundreds of millions of humans who are living in other dimensions. So, until a further time when I should like to be of service to you, I remain your brother,

— Volta

CHAPTER 81

Greetings, fellow earth men.

As is the custom, in beginning a transmission to identify one's self, I shall follow the decorum by telling you I am an individual who was identified upon the earth during the Grecian or Hellenic period of time, by the name of Hippocrates. It is said that I had something to do with the parental birth of the science of medicine. However, I can only emphasize that in some of the sciences and philosophies, much credit was given to individuals which was not fully justified. There has also been a great deal of work in the field of medicine which has come from much more highly developed and illustrious minds than mine.

As an individual serving mankind here in the second section of Parhelion, I am privileged to be something of a teacher in one of the very large classrooms into which you shall go directly and become somewhat acquainted with what is going on in that section of teaching. In the previous transmission, you were partially introduced to this section, but for the purpose of reacquainting your concepts of this section, we shall again begin at the front portico, or doorway.

This huge opening is about one hundred feet high. As you see, it looks something like the huge mouth of a dragon, because it is armed with great prisms of crystal material all around the outside periphery. Beautiful streamers of light are passing through these prisms, in something like a curtain of rainbow light through which you will walk directly. Overhead, on the top of this great archway, is a symbol of two interlocked triangles which denotes our capacity of servitude to mankind in general.

Now let us step back through this beautiful, radiating and pulsating curtain of energy, but it will not harm you. We shall go directly into what might be called, in the language which you best understand, the foyer of this great section, or the central entrance similar to the lobby of a huge hotel; or, perhaps it looks more like one of the huge railroad stations in your time and dimension.

This great central portion is so large that it could easily house a small community. As you look at your feet, you will see that you are stepping on a carpet of soft and beautiful radiant energy, which is somewhat like a mystic cloud of ectoplasm. Directly in the middle of this beautiful central or circular dimension is a huge fountain which is simultaneously spouting in all directions, streams of beautiful radiant energy similar to water, and seems to be expanding and receding, pulsating and falling about in numerous cascades and rivulets, which is beautiful beyond description.

Above you, and that which you call a ceiling, is actually a very beautiful blue vault of pulsating, radiant energy, and is interlocked in the structures of the prisms and dimensions with which you have now become familiar. All of this great, beautiful center section is almost as radiant and pulsating as the curtain of energy through which you just walked.

The lengthy discussion covering the atom was necessary, as was the transmission which acquainted you with the different types and frequencies of wave forms existing in the various dimensions of perception about you at all times; for God is the ultimate

757

source of energy, and He infinitely expresses Himself as energy in one form or another in all of the dimensions and in an infinite number of ways.

In going into this particular classroom, we shall see something which is similar in many respects to the fifth center of Parhelion, where the higher order of spiritual therapy and healing was being conducted in conjunction with the planet Venus. It is quite obvious to you by now, that we have to teach a great number of students and that there must be a great deal of coming and going with the hundreds of thousands and millions of students, who come and go through these centers. They, in themselves, must be at least Initiates or in some high order of frequency or vibration before they can enter into these dimensions. By necessity, therefore, there is a vast and infinite number of seemingly reproductive processes which might parallel or similarize our sections into somewhat likened proportions.

Now let us step through this huge doorway into the section with which I am very familiar, since I have been here for something like several hundred years in earth time. Here you will see various and sundry types of therapies, of diagnoses and healing, as they are, and will be practiced by the different terrestrial and astral dimensions, where man is residing in his evolutionary flight into the higher dimensions.

Let us step over to this section, for instance, and see this huge room. If you will pardon me for a moment, I shall describe it for the benefit of the reader who has not the opportunity of seeing it with his spiritual eyes as do you. Like many classrooms which you have seen, it is so vast in proportion, that one of your largest cities could very easily be placed in the center of it, with plenty of room to expand. In the different sections of this huge room, you will see groups of students who are associated with rather peculiar and weird looking apparatus. You will notice also as we go into these different sections in this classroom that the apparatus connected with each is entirely different. Very obviously because we lack time, and because you might become unbalanced in trying to follow the descriptions of these numerous and thousands of different types of electronic equipment, we shall merely take a short cut and confine our explorations to the dimension which is the most relative to the earth at this time.

Therefore, we shall go into this section which is devoted to a type of diagnosis which is entirely electronic by nature. Here before you, you see a group of students who are very intently watching the psychic body of an individual which is being diagnosed for some types of conditions which are existing in his psychic structures.

May I digress for a moment and tell you that the patients or individuals who are brought here for treatment, are all in their psychic forms of consciousness just as they were in the other sections of Parhelion, or in Venus itself. I might also point out to you, that in order to bring these people here, there must be some very definite reason for so doing. It isn't that we just forage around and pick up whatever we can. The relatives and friends of every person, or the person himself, must in some way be vitally connected with a great purpose and good to mankind. If the friends and relatives of the individual are strong enough in their mental purpose and in their situation so they can extend thoughts or wishes of good will, or if the assuredness of the person's own spiritual qualities is sufficiently strong, then those are the necessary ingredients which enable us to contact the individual who has lost his flesh; consequently, we pick up his malformed psychic spiritual body and bring it here for treatment as was done in the fifth section.

The treatments here are of a slightly different nature to a large degree, inasmuch as we remove many of the mental obsessions, or the obsessive entities directly from the psychic bodies of the individuals. In looking at this apparatus which you see directly before you, you will find it somewhat reminiscent of a large television screen. You will see the teacher attaching different types of electrodes directly to the different centers of the psychic body, such as the soles of the feet, the palms of the hands, the solar plexus, the front of the forehead, and the different regions of the spine, such as the medulla oblongata.

As the teacher deftly manipulates a number of dials, you will see different types of wave forms emerging on the screen of this huge television set. These wave forms, which flash into view in a very magnified proportion, are the exact wave forms which existed in the person's body, except that they were magnified somewhat like an electronic microscope. As he goes from condition to condition, the teacher points out just what these wave forms mean and gives their interpretation.

I would say to you doctors and physicians on the earth at this time, that you are approaching the threshold of inventive genius in electronics, which will, in a few hundred years or less, produce this science which we are displaying here. Already in your laboratories and clinics you have some apparatus of electronic nature which can diagnose, to some degree, the condition of the human body in an electronic fashion. The X-ray machine was the first of these electronic instruments which cast certain shadows upon the photographic plate from a fluorescent screen.

You also have such instruments as the electroencephalograph, which records brain waves and the electrocardiograph, which denotes the pulsations of the heart—as well as the influence upon the heart—onto a fluorescent screen, called an oscilloscope. However, to develop the science which could develop the electronic apparatus similar to that used here, would entail much more science than you now possess on the earth. It would also be mandatory that you know of the psychic structures of the human individual as he exists on earth and as he is connected with the higher dimensions. It is quite obvious that you could not invent a machine for which you did not know the purpose.

Now I am going to make a very strong statement to you doctors: there is no condition (and there are no exceptions), known in medicine which is not *first* produced in the psychic body of the individual through some malformation of psychic structures. The very intent or purpose of the organic chemistry of the body is supported in the dimension of not only atomic frequencies, but also in that which is called the centers of the chakras, as they express the life forces into the body of the individual. Any misalignment, either in the atomic structures, or in the expression of energies through the chakras or in any other way in which the psychic body is so connected with the individual, has direct repercussions into the physical flesh or the condition of health of the individual.

Even the person who breaks his leg cannot term it as an accident; instead it can be traced as a negation to some obstructive force in the process of his thinking. If he had been completely positive, he would not have broken his leg. There is absolutely *no* condition which you can name, that I could not point out as the result of some type of misalignment or negative condition which existed in the person's mentality; or he might be said to have obstructed and misaligned the forces which made his life possible in his existence in the terrestrial dimension.

Later we shall go into different factional orders and we shall peer somewhat into the different portions of the psychic body to see just what happens to the wave forms and what malformations are incurred by the use of drugs or anaesthetics, or even through some of the more popular and very widely sold analgesic sedatives of earth today, which are known as bromides or aspirin. Pain, or the symptoms of pain, as expressed in the human body is merely nature's way, or your own intelligence, of crying out in a very definite fashion that there is something wrong with you.

To rush to the medicine cabinet and swallow a couple of pills is very wrong. It is detrimental in two different ways: first you incur some sort of palliative relief from your pain. This immediately disconnects you from any further purpose, as far as you are concerned, in getting to the basic cause of the pain and eliminating it. The basic cause is always just beyond the horizon of your thinking, and goes into the superstructure of your psychic body.

If you have pains or malformed conditions in your body, they are very definite symptoms that you are misaligned somewhere along the line of transmission from the Supreme Powerhouse, which we shall call God, in which case it is best that you take stock of yourself and put these things back into alignment.

Now, of course, it is easy to suggest things to people, but it is very difficult if we try to point out cures. Cures in themselves are comparatively simple in nature and surprisingly so. If the reader would digest even partially, the concepts of this book and the knowledge and wisdom which is contained within its pages, we could very safely guarantee that he would, in a very short period of time, feel the results and the repercussions of this new knowledge and wisdom, not only in his body, but in his daily life. In the years to come, and in his future reincarnations and evolutions, he would realize more and more the impact of impounding the principles of wisdom and truth which we are trying to explain.

The average individual, as he exists in the earth dimension today, reminds us somewhat of a man who has been locked in a completely darkened room. In trying to escape he becomes frantic and rushes blindly about, butting his head and body against the walls and injuring himself. It would be much more logical if he would go quietly about the room until, with his fingers, he found the doorway, and thus unlock the door and step out into the daylight.

You must always remember that you are largely responsible for everything you do which comes to you as an experience in your daily existence. As was previously stated, you sometimes become an unwilling victim in your ignorance. The earth-like translations of law say definitely that ignorance is no excuse. If a person steps into his automobile to go to a certain destination and is inadvertently involved in an automobile accident, wherein one or two persons die and others are injured, he is technically guilty of manslaughter, and he will be hauled before the courts. However, theoretically, this person is not guilty. No one in his right mind would set out deliberately to commit so felonious an assault against his neighbor.

We can say that this is very much the case with the average individual; he lacks the common ingredients of intelligence in knowing the basic laws of evolution and reincarnation. As such a person, after so-called death, passes into whatever doorway is most conveniently presented to him and which he feels to be most compatible to his rate of vibration at the moment. He may find himself in a strange world which is entirely unsuited to him. It may develop farther along the line that he may incur a great shock or a psychic impact of such a nature and intensity, that as he reincarnates into a future lifetime, he may hang more or less suspended between the two worlds and will vainly try to reorient himself into his own consciousness from either one or the other dimension. Such a person is termed in the language of psychiatry in your world as a schizophrenic. Other types of insanity to which this section is devoted, are conditions which are called manic-depressives or dementia praecox; but whatever term the scientist or doctor uses for these mental aberrations, many of them are much more than any diagnostician on your earth today can even faintly visualize.

To show you what we mean, we shall step over into this section which is rather close to the one we have just visited, to witness a diagnosis. Stepping over to the table, you will see what looks like the psychic form of an individual. The name or sex is immaterial; but looking closely you will see that hanging from the portion of that which is commonly called the naval, is a large, rather ugly looking object which looks something like a fat slug, or a leech, or a bloodsucker. This is actually an adhesion or an obsession which attached itself to this man's psychic body in his earth life. The man died in an asylum as a violently insane person, for this bloodsucker or leechlike creature was sucking at the very vital basis of his psychic nature, and thus so misaligned and distorted the psychic, that in such a state, he had no semblance of sanity.

As was pointed out to you by Pearce and several others, that mental adhesions or obsessions are of two different natures; the one just discussed is compounded by the factions of negative thinking, called thought form obsessions, like the one you see here hanging from this individual's psychic center, which is called the solar plexus, or the umbilical cord of his spiritual nature. It was the constant repetitious acts and consequences in his negative state of consciousness on the earth which generated this huge bloodsucker-like creature which was hanging from him and devitalizing him and making him what he was.

Later on the teachers or the doctors of this center will approach and attach proper electrodes to this creature so that it will be properly rectified and passed off into the oblivion of energy. Thus the man will be freed and he will be enabled to return to some dimension for a future reincarnation where he will be, or rather shall I say, he will allow himself the privilege of proving to his superconscious self that he is a creature of infinite origin.

As was pointed out to you in the fifth section, many of these creatures or obsessions were horrible beyond description. Now we shall look at some more of the thought-form body adhesive types of obsessions which attach themselves to people. Here is an individual who had the incurable habit of cigarette smoking. You will see something of the same form of a leech-like creature hanging from the back portion of his brain, called the medulla oblongata. This creature, too, is obstructing a very natural sequence of purpose of energy transference into the individual's body. You will also notice that other extrusions or masses are forming up and down the person's spine in the different portions which relate themselves to different fractions of psychic centers. In time, had the individual lived, these would have become somewhat like that leech-like creature which was sucking the

energies and life forces from the individual mentioned earlier.

We could go on and on with these obsessions
which are thought-form bodies, such as are attached
to alcoholics. The whole picture in many cases, however, is not complete for here we have other types of
obsessions. A person who has been the victim of such
an obsessive form, usually has also some other entities which are actual human beings in a discarnate
expression, who were alcoholics.

Here before us you will see an alcoholic. But, before we could remove him to this section of the classroom for treatment, we had to remove at least a
hundred or so attachments, which were entities and
all of whom had been alcoholics in previous reincarnations on the earth. They had clustered around this
individual to such an extent that he was literally
buried by them, so deeply that we had to dig down
and remove them from him before we could find him
at the bottom of the pile. This individual I would say,
died from what, on earth, is commonly termed the
delirium tremens.

I see, however, that your psychic centers are becoming shaken with what is being revealed to you. So
I believe that we had better rest for a while until we
can be further reconstituted and re-energized and
thus return to the exploration of the center.

We are most anxious that the average individual—
be he layman or Truth seeker, as well as the physician—might examine truly, in the light of truth, just
exactly what exists with many of the poor souls who
so greatly need help and counsel in the doctor's office
or clinic; even those who go to the hospital and suffer
the mental torture of the operative treatment, which
removes only the *effect* of some condition deeply
rooted in the psychic centers of the individual, and

are beyond the reach of the scalpel. Such a condition cannot possibly be sutured so that it does not again break open and inflict some sort of pain or torture into the individual in some future day.

The only permanent and successful corrective therapy in these treatments is the removal of the negation from the place in which the disease exists, *which is within the psychic body of the individual himself.* It cannot be done simply from the physical or exterior portion of his body, where the effects manifest themselves in the greatest proportion and abundance. However, let us rest a while.

Now that we are rested, let us resume. But, before we go directly into the business of viewing some of the activities here in this section—which we have called a ward—several questions have arisen in your mind which should be answered before further progress is made. I previously made a very emphatic statement, that no conditions are to be found in the human body which do not have their origin or their linkage in the psychic consciousness of the psychic self of the individual.

The average earth doctor will say: "Well, what about the micro-organisms known as bacteria or the pathogenic disease germs?" There is much evidence in your histories which would directly answer this question without my pointing out various and objective facts which are very pertinent. I might begin first by reminding you of the man of Galilee, known as Jesus, who never knew a sick day in his life. He could step up to the leper, or to any person with any condition and that person would be healed instantly. It is obvious after a moment's thought, that this person's body was so infused with some sort of Infinite Light or vibration, that germs just simply couldn't live in contact with Him. In the daily manifestation of life on the earth, in every individual there is a great deal of preconditioning. He is preconditioned at birth to accept, in the reactionary order of life, various types of conditions which he finds at a later date he must have removed from his consciousness before he can evolve into a future dimension.

The acceptance of pathogenic organisms or diseases into the body is one of these preconditioned notions which have no actual foundation in the true spiritual consciousness of the individual. If man could place this point firmly in his mind and so condition himself against any and all such invasions of pathogenic organisms, he could, by knowing of the higher dimensions of frequency relationship, so infuse his body with Infinite Radiant Light, as did Jesus, that he would make himself immune to any conditions which he might incur upon the earth.

To go a little farther, if man would study the Eastern philosophies of India, he would find many Yogis who have existed, and who still exist—Holy men who have gone entire lifetimes in all sorts of conditions and places—among the very sewer places which would be the origin of many of the great plagues of mankind, such as the bubonic plague, which at one time swept over Europe in the Middle Ages and decimated whole populations.

Here again is a curious fact. Many of the people who took out the dead bodies of the plague-stricken victims were themselves untouched and immune to this disease. Where did they derive their immunity? They were not vaccinated nor were they preconditioned against this disease. It was obvious that they had, in some way, incurred immunity to a large degree by the faith which absolved them from the contact of the pathogene of the bubonic plague organism.

Another question which might arise, is how we are

linked to these vital forces which have been explained to us in numerous ways; forces that we might contact as they stem into our bodies. If we may point out an allegory, we may better explain our point. The small watch which you wear on your wrist, or is enclosed in the pocket of your vest, contains a large spring which is called the main-spring. Through a series of small gears or wheels—which are notched on the edges—the energy from the main-spring, as it is wound up, in turn, turns these small notched wheels with the end result that there is a balance wheel and an escape movement which is motivated by a fulcrum and lever.

Your life can be somewhat similarized. Your prime and motivating force, which is called a mainspring, is contained in the great Life Cycle or the Superconsciousness of the individual. Through various other differences in fractional divisions of energy transference which relates you to these higher dimensions, such as the atomic structures of your body, the intuitive faculties of your own mind link you with the higher constructive elements of the psychic body similar to the process of the notched wheels of the watch.

Your own emotional difference in the happenstance of everyday life is something like the oscillating balance wheel of the watch, and the escape movement is in your own consciousness which is your value and your equation of your personal sense in your relationship to your fellow men about you. The difference here is that instead of having notched wheels, we are linked to the higher motivating forces in our lives by the frequency or harmonic relationship as it has been so adequately explained to you.

Another question may arise in the mind of the individual: if the atomic structures in the body are supported by higher dimensions, why then is it necessary to eat? My dear friends, it is not necessary to eat. Here again is a great deal of preconditioning in the body. Man has accepted the fact and so constituted his body with the alimentary canal and various other organic methods of assimilation simply by preconditioning. The body, in its entirety, is in a sense directly the result of such preconditioning and such ideas.

I would point out to you that there are actual, authenticated case histories of many people on the earth who have lived for many years without food passing their lips. In the act of eating, you are merely taking into your body another dimension of atomic energy, since all food dissolves into atomic structures similar to the structures in your body. Thus you are merely combining in your body another element or dimension of atomic energy.

Sooner or later, in your evolution, you will completely dissociate yourself from the idea that eating is necessary. And in doing so, your body will begin to function in another dimension, whereby the energies of its nature come in a much greater abundance and through the more natural channels of emergence in the various psychic centers of your body. You will, just as was demonstrated in the Bible, literally be fed by the ravens; the ravens of course were not actual or real. The men who wrote the Bible simply had to understand these things in their own way; so they said the ravens fed the man, but as in the case of many Avatars, or men of a more highly developed nature, they have found ways and means of infusing into their bodies, the elements which are necessary for the maintenance of these atomic structures.

If we think for a moment, is it not logical that since the atoms themselves are merely products of a higher dimension and are supported by such energies, if we have the wisdom and the intelligence to further propagate this understanding, then food will become entirely unnecessary? This is all in itself a part of your own spiritual progression and growth, principles which you will gradually infuse into the construction of your psychic body, gradually displacing the older vibrations which are merely preconditioned concepts of materialism and material values, as they exist about you in your earth life. This is the primary purpose of reincarnation, inasmuch as a house cannot be built without a foundation. So if man is to be a man, he must understand who he is, and how he comes into existence, and this naturally must follow from the very lowest order of conception into the very highest.

Man cannot visualize himself or his fellow men in any portion or in his entirety until he himself has walked through the same pathway of experience and so has taken unto himself the knowledge and wisdom of the occurrence of the emotional experience. As has been told to you, the experience itself is of no consequence. Experience is Infinite in nature, and it is merely the way in which you relate yourself to the experience. In the direct proportion as you relate yourself to experience, so is the need of the Superconsciousness projected into your consciousness; thus you automatically select according to the proportion in which you are able to achieve the elements of these emotional experiences.

Some people say that God will never give man a problem larger than he is able to solve. It would be more correct to say that a man would never give unto himself, anything which he is unable to solve. It is *NOT* the Immutable Ever-present and Omnipotent God Force which selects or determines any one particular quotient of experience or emotionalism in our lives. *We Ourselves* are acting as an agent and select in proportion to that which we have either preconditioned for ourselves, or into which we can evolve in the natural sequence and order of logic and reason, as we have so propounded and impounded these virtues in our psychic experiences.

Now you have formed somewhat of an idea of the watch, the balance wheel, and the numerous gears; and that you are somehow linked in this manner with the vibratory mechanisms of these higher dimensions to God Himself. So, we shall begin to understand how it is that hypnotism can exist. Hypnotism merely means that another individual's mind (the hypnotist's) slips in somewhere between these gears or the Life Cycle of the individual's conscious mind, because the conscious mind is the balance wheel. It was also similarized as the experiences of the subconscious, as they are contained in the psychic vortexes and wave lengths of the individual; and each act and each consequence merely flashes in the mind, just as on the television screen, the various relative factors which involve these emotional experiences.

Every individual immediately tunes himself in, as it were, or there flashes in his conscious mind, the result, or the psychic impact, of any one or a dozen, or perhaps a hundred such emotional experiences. He thus compounds his immediate actions as a direct result of such reactionary values of the impounding and the derivatives of such emotionalism.

The subconscious mind can therefore be said to not always be productive of the most reasonable and logical equations in man's lifetime. As a consequence, the individual can likewise be said to be unable to think constructively, or we say that he is not a clear thinker. This statement is quite true. The average individual, unless he is clairvoyant or well trained, cannot link himself up—as you are doing—to become the subject of some higher and more intelligent forces, with which the Celestial Universes of God abound so abundantly.

The mere fact that man, at numerous times, brings expressions into his world which are indicative of realistic and creative genius far in advance of his time, proves conclusively the principles of clairvoyance, which are an invaluable adjunct to the process of constructive thinking. It becomes quite clearly apparent that in this process he has linked himself in a clairvoyant fashion to the higher dimensions of his consciousness.

This was the principle used by Sir Isaac Newton who, in sitting in meditation, linked himself with the higher dimensions and impounded these various constructive ideas in his mind, which he later wrote down. By reading his biography you will know that his concepts were far in advance of his time. The same principles and processes of development can be applied to every person who may become what is called a constructive thinker, and thus may add something to the posterity of mankind. In a sense, the objective or conscious mind of the individual is not a thinking mechanism. It is a correlative mechanism which merely relates and rerelates man to the emotional experiences of his past lives. The pure tenet of constructive thinking lies within the domain of the superconsciousness and relates the mind to the Infinite Wisdom of God's Nature.

Let us return for a moment to that great center in which we were previously examining the various spiritual malefactors of those individuals who have perverted their domain of progression to the point where they became atrophied or obsessed with certain conditions.

In this section is a woman who was quite recently brought here with a rather compounded condition of both thought and entity obsessions. Her history began on the earth many years ago. When she had arrived somewhere past the middle age of her life, the passing of her husband left her feeling very keenly the loss of his love and companionship; and knowing nothing of the spiritual worlds and dimensions, for several years she grieved insufferably for him. She thus constructed in her mind a thought-form body, which became very adhesively related to her own psychic structures. Now, such unbalanced conditions in the psychic natures of people have somewhat of a way of leveling off, or of finding a point of balance, or as we call it, a valence. So it was that to divert her from a sure course of insanity, the forces which were directly linked to her nature and which were helping her, created the condition within her mind that made her somewhat of a hypochondriac.

In other words, she began developing numerous physical symptoms of pain, or the consciousness that she was disturbed by the fact that she was ill. This did indeed take her mind off the influence of the thought-form of her husband; and she began making many trips back and forth to numerous doctors who did, or did not satisfy her own immediate needs of diagnosis.

There was one particular practitioner who went so far as to anesthetize her and make an initial incision in her abdomen, even though there was nothing wrong with her. Immediately following the operation she recovered from an imaginary illness which cost her a great sum of money. But, as it so developed, these obsessive processes became more and more developed so that she began to attract unto herself, other similar entities who were vibrating in such harmonious conjunction with her own state of consciousness, and that when she was brought here, she had a dozen or so of these retarded and malformed entities hovering about her, who had torn shreds from her psychic body and had entwined themselves into these shreds.

We had very carefully to remove these obsessive entities and return them to their respective positions. We had also to remove the psychic obsessions of the thought-form body, which was supposedly her husband. He, himself, was instrumental in bringing about this whole treatment as he was somewhat of an advanced soul who had lived many years in a spiritual dimension before his passing. He was able to be very constructively useful in bringing about a more happy and satisfactory conclusion to this case. Now her psychic body will be returned to an astral world with him, into such a dimension where he will be able gradually to infiltrate into her consciousness the necessary ingredients of thought and consciousness which will enable her to function properly in that dimension. Later on, she may wish to reincarnate into the world thereby enabling her more strongly to reinforce the psychic structures of her body and to reinstate herself into the natural sequence of her evolution.

Let us go a little further into the concepts of hypnotism. It can be, and is something quite useful as an adjunct to the position or doctrine of your earth at this time; for anesthesia in the form of hypnotism is gradually being used in dentistry and in numerous other types of corrective therapies which involve certain dissections of the body which induce a great deal of pain into the consciousness of the individual.

Many persons are highly susceptible to the effects of anesthesia, for as every doctor knows, different types of anesthesia must be used in individual cases. The effect of anesthesia in itself is something on the order of hypnosis, inasmuch as a drug, or a violently agitated atomic structure, is interjected into the normal process of, shall I say, the little wheels in the watch or the cycle of the conscious expression of the individual. The highly agitated atomic structure, known as ether, is similar to the propane solvents contained in other types of anesthetics.

The nitrous oxide, which is used by the dentist, has some such similar effect; its whole effect, however, lies strictly in the domain of disrupting the natural continuity of cycles, which permits the conscious correlation of existence into the objective mind of the individual. The impact of these drugs and the natural disruption, or the continuity of psychic disruption, often brings about rather drastic results. These results may or may not be immediately felt by the person who was subjected to the effects of these anesthetic agents.

If you will think for a moment, you will see that it is a case of psychical transference into the objective consciousness of the individual and that it must resolve itself into dimensional factors, or frequency vibrations. But there must also be an element of synchronization, otherwise the individual could not properly integrate the faculty of memory or conscious experience into the emotional impact as he has so lived in his various experiences.

This lack of synchronization happens many times in the cases of individuals who have been anesthetized. In some future day some such synchronization and counter-synchronization may be set up in these vibratory structures of his nature so that he may become out of tune or alignment with himself. A more advanced and more easily understood case of lack of synchronization is sometimes called senility, or the disease of the mentally aged people, who sometimes lack a great deal of the coordinative relationships in their daily lives. Some of the wheels in their vibratory structures are spinning madly; others are at a standstill for lack of proper cohesive vibratory relationship. Consequently, they are unable to factually relate experience with experience in a proportionate or a balanced form, as it might be expressed in the balance wheel of the watch.

We have the old adage or axiom, "An ounce of prevention is worth a pound of cure." You pride yourself that your country is the most advanced and cultured nation in the world. However, this is an idea which is subject to a great deal of variation in examining the statistics of the mental levels and conditions of the people as they exist in America today.

Basically the ideals of your country were motivated by the very highest principles of spiritual inception. The men who compounded the Constitution of the United States were infused with a great humanitarian plan of action. They, in themselves, expressed a great deal of this higher idealism in their daily lives, and this infusion inspired them with their zeal in writing the Declaration of Independence, and in severing the relationship with the mother country of England. However, after constituting the United States, they very quickly found that there were many people living in the world who did not completely justify all of the principles which were impounded in this Declaration of Independence. Therefore, it became necessary with the passing of years to circumscribe certain limits of action into the dimensions of expression in the individual life as it existed in the various states which constituted the country. These became known as amendments.

The first ten became the Bill of Rights. There were further additions or amendments to the Constitution which number, I believe, about twenty-two, counting the repeal of the Volstead Act. As history developed, and as the size of the country increased, so did the complexities of the civilization. Various civic and state governmental branches, orders of legislation, and branches of judicial execution sprang into being to legislate or to enact laws, with the judicial branch to enforce these laws. Further enforcement was supplemented by the various police departments. As the years rolled by, the complexities of this governmental system increased. Because the system was based strictly upon the reactionary order of thinking that a man was not guilty until he was convicted of crime; therefore, the individual was allowed, without training and without thought, promiscuously to exploit his own dominion or his own domain of thought into whatever direction he conceived; if he were clever enough to contrive this beyond the eye or the ear of some law abiding agency, he could further his own interests and his own gain.

As a result, at the present time, the average citizen of the United States is under the jurisdiction of at least six or seven thousand different laws, which exist in the statutes of different state and governmental orders. It is obvious that under such a governmental system, there is going to be a great deal of confusion, duplication and, as a consequence, a great deal of error. We all know, factually, that there are innocent men and women in penitentiaries, and that there are many felons who are walking the streets and who should, by the token of your own understanding, be incarcerated in place of the innocent victims.

However, the basic and motivating forces behind law and order are always justifiable in their outward expression because man is so constituted in the higher dominion of his conscious nature, that he does not willfully become a malefactor towards his fellow man. The point which I am making here is that the numerous complications of governmental orders and factions, the natural sequence of error, exploitation, and other elements which have entered into the construction of what is called your democracy, have been indeed something which is puzzling to the average individual. He has been forced to compromise himself and his own natural order of conscience or his self-esteem into these various relations and integrations of the governmental system. He knows, just as everyone does, that there is a great deal of malpractice which is going on behind the front of self-respect.

With all the consequence of these various compromises, the individual is also confronted by a great deal of what can be called exploitation, as I have mentioned before. He is subjected to innumerable pressures from within and without his own household. These relate him to the various obligations which are incurred in living in the community or city in which he has so chosen to reside. The order of taxation, or the supporting of the governmental systems and the burdens which they incur, are to the individual, very oppressive. All in all, it can be said that civilization, or democracy as you are now supposedly enjoying it, is one which presents such a vast multitude of intricate systems of expression that the average individual has become partially if not extremely, neurotic.

According to the statistics which are available to the average individual, it is estimated conservatively that one in sixteen is in need of some psychiatric treatment. The question which is posed in my mind is: would this psychiatric treatment, with the methods which are in use today in your country, do the individual any good? They are only a step removed from the cage and the iron-barred cell. Your psychiatry is extremely primitive even in what you call your advanced state. In the future day and evolution, as man develops psychiatric systems of therapy from the spiritual dimensions, he will begin to see just exactly how crude these methods and systems are.

Simply to remove a patient from the immediate environment of the systems of various oppressions which have occurred in his daily life, does not mean that he is necessarily entitled to a quick and permanent cure. The breaking of the various psychical factions of emotions and the removal of these pressures, will not necessarily remove the emotional experience from his psychic body. These are impounded into the robot-like existence of everyday life, in which he has incurred a neurosis, in wave forms and dimensions, which do not ordinarily respond to such reactionary treatment.

A patient who is thus removed into another environment, and who seeks his own means to escape the pressures which have induced his neurosis or his mental aberration, will, to some extent and to some degree, relieve himself automatically with the temporary removal of these pressures. However, he must return some day to the status quo of his civilization from whence he emerged. He will then re-incur the same pressures in different forms, and quite likely he will revert into an even more aborted mental state of aberration.

The question which probably by now is posed in your mind is, then, what governmental system will be a panacea for all man's ills? The answer is very direct and conclusive: there is no governmental system which has ever been in existence on the earth, or that will ever be in existence on the earth, which will be a panacea for man's ills.

The dimension of curative values, as they must enter into the individual concept, must come from within the individual himself with the evaluation of his consciousness into domains of constructive thought and evaluations which, while impounded into his nature, will so relate him with the higher dimensions of force and action, that the various inadequacies of governmental systems, of community life, and social structures will vanish. They will be replaced by higher orders and concepts of social structures which will further integrate into a higher order of the dominant factors of man's spiritual nature.

In regard to the various intricate electronic equipment which you have at least partially seen and witnessed in operation, I might say to the physician and psychiatrist on the earth, that there are machines in actual use in different earth or terrestrial dimensions, which are somewhat advanced to your own earth. We might point out Mars, for instance; there, a great deal of this corrective therapy is done from the spiritual side of life by merely recognizing the super-consciousness of the individual and in relating and relinking himself to the higher dimensions of consciousness.

The continuity or expression of physical waves of form and motion which are impounded within the psychic body can be changed or neutralized to some, or to a large extent by the mere application of superimposed frequencies of somewhat more than a supersonic nature. Such vortexes as may reside which can give the criminal tendencies or their propensities to an individual, are thus removed, as well as such obstacles or vortexes which can be called blocks in his consciousness or evaluations which were incurred in previous reincarnations. The individual then feels extremely free in his own dimension to move about and factually integrate himself in his evolutions.

May I say that I sincerely appreciate the fact of coming to you and somewhat expounding some of the concepts from the centers of Shamballa which are more or less directly within and conceived within the dimensions of our own consciousness. The things which are in order and in sequence in our daily lives, if I can call them "daily lives," in our existence here in the Shamballas, are orders of artifacts which are beyond your conception in a finite dimension. The nature of the miracles which were performed by Jesus would also be quite elemental if you could see the nature of what you might call miracles in the natural functioning of our daily lives here in these centers.

These centers themselves defy description; so likewise do the faculties of expression in the order of teaching and learning, for you are either a student or a teacher, but you are neither all of the time learning nor are you all of the time teaching, since one becomes the other and that is the way we progress. We are expressing here, too, the concepts of polarity by accepting and giving. This, in your daily lives, would be a concept which could be of great value to the individual of the earth. If everyone on the little planet on which you are now living could devote at least an hour of his day to extending all of the virtues of his personality in a constructive way toward his fellow man, the order of the earth would be changed in a very short time. Armies, navies, and wars would quickly disappear; likewise would disappear much of the disease and pestilence which you have infused and accepted into the domain of your daily existence.

However, I see that the vocal chords of the channel are beginning to become a little tired, so I must let him rest until either myself or some other one of us here comes in to lead him further into the field of exploration in this central section.

Your humble servant,

— Hippocrates

CHAPTER 82

Greetings again, dear ones. We are most happy to resume our explorations; but we would first like to extend to you our deepest regrets that you were so discomforted by witnessing the removal, and the adhesive qualities, of the various obsessions in some of the cases which were under therapeutic care in the previous exploration. (We Ernest and Ruth, were both physically nauseated after the viewing). In the future, we will try to keep you from feeling the full impact of witnessing any such kindred happenings.

In our previous explorations, and in our general discussion of governmental orders and transmission of laws and social conduct in the great country of America, we were not criticizing instead we were objectively pointing out that which could be such obvious derelictions of purpose in the execution of governmental orders as might well cause a prema-ture and decadent condition in your civilization.

As was first pointed out, the Constitution of the United States was so morally and spiritually inspired and contrived in the development of the history of the country, that in a theoretical sense, the citizen should enjoy a great deal of social, moral and spiritual freedom. Due to the numerous legislative and judicial bodies which, according to their collective and individual interpretation of such moral and spiritual virtues as may be contained in the individual's life, some of the original virtues of the Constitution and its moral and spiritual principles have been some-what lost. The average citizen who would like to lead a decent and moral life, knows that such a pathway is somewhat straight and narrow. His course of action in the maze and intricacies of the numerous laws, in the legislation and in the execution of them, is such that his course of conduct necessarily must be clearly defined. He knows that should he ever inadvertently become involved in some legal presupposition, the outcome of such an entanglement will depend largely upon the amount of money he is able to spend and the ability and brains of the legal advice which he is able to hire.

These things in themselves, and their aspects, have a very definite impact on the daily life and conduct of the average American citizen. While he is basically motivated by his own individual moral concepts, yet he knows that to the right and left of him are indi-viduals who are pursuing their course of life to the extreme confines of any elasticity which may be con-tained in the interpretation of the numerous laws under which the various civic and governmental orders are functioning at that moment.

He in himself is therefore somewhat morally shocked by the depredations of these individuals and by their numerous devious pathways and exploita-tions. All of these things are a sort of compound of various moral fears. In not having his course of action too clearly defined, man may thus be shatter-ed by the constant companion of fear, since his own sense of moral justice is so continually outraged and he is made indignant by the cost of the exploitations of the various individualistic and other types of inter-pretation.

He may see in the political issues which involve elections, a great deal of what is termed "mud-slinging." He may also be quite cognizant that there is a great deal of immorality, which is called gangland, or underworld activity. He also knows that there are great negative forces and pressures on the outside of his world, as well as within his own country, which are striving to undermine and overthrow whatever structures of moral conduct and decency the people have been able to achieve. The powers across the sea are shipping in great quantities of various types of drugs, with the intent of demoralizing and overthrowing the moral precepts of the people. Incidentally, I would like to point out to the leaders of your nation that they would be very wise if they would spend less on army and navy expenditures and devote more of the money to such governmental agencies as would suppress this extremely dangerous activity which is going on at an accelerated rate in your country today.

There is also, shall I say, another type of propaganda existing in your nation which is in itself demoralizing, for it is somewhat of an opiate. Statistics show the very low rate of activity in the various elections and in the functions of electing the various governmental enforcement agencies. This apathy as such is very dangerous in itself. It is an indication, or a symptom, that the public is rather indifferent to the general trend of the times. This indifference can be generally summarized under the heading of shock. The average individual, in the transitions of his daily life, has become so involved with the numerous compromises and complexities of his intricate way of life, that he is somewhat shocked into a condition of apathy.

The various political factions, or parties which are involved in the governmental orders, are in themselves guilty of a great deal of misconduct, in the fact that they very frequently publicize propaganda which is both misleading and often wrongly slanted. This is done—more or less—to instill a sort of a feeling in the general trend of public opinion that the party in particular, which is in power and functioning as the governmental head of the nation, is the most efficient of the several parties which may, or may not, be elected into power in the next general election.

The citizen, too is somewhat confused by the apparent derelictions in statistics in relation to public health. He is told in the various newspapers and other systems of communication that, in general, the life expectancy of the individual has been increased by a number of years, or that public health is, to a certain extent, a great deal better than it was in such and such a time.

Statistics such as these are in themselves quite dangerous as they are often contrasted for the purpose of the campaigning which is being done in the numerous solicitations of charitable health organizations. These organizations are, in their own way, devoted to corrective therapies in the numerous types of illnesses, which are somewhat the product of your civilization. Within his own home, in his daily walk of life in the streets, factories, or offices where he works, the citizen is continually solicited and made aware of a great deal of public disease and ill health. He is sometimes quite shocked when the actual statistics of these conditions are revealed to him.

He is constantly made aware of the conditions of cancer, tuberculosis, multiple sclerosis and various other diseases, which have their origin in the highly conceived way of civilization. The processing which is done in the foods and in the outlets of the various productive sources from which the citizen draws in the ways and means of daily life, are in themselves so highly synthesized that often the foods do not contain the necessary organic or nutritional values which properly sustain his life.

The viewer is constantly seeing upon the screen of his television set or in his daily newspapers a great hue and cry, urging him immediately to consult his physician upon certain symptoms, or he is solicited to contribute what is drastically needed for the various types of mental or physical afflictions. The truth of the matter is, that in the general consensus of analysis of these numerous and conflicting facets of his everyday life, the average individual very quickly becomes either frustrated and neurotic, or he assumes rather an indifferent and apathetic attitude toward these various types of conflicts. The mere fact that he may assume an apathetic attitude does not necessarily guarantee immunity from these conflictions, for he is quite aware of them at all times, whether or not he acknowledges them in the more superficial threshold of his own mind.

In walking about the streets and in his various activities, man is constantly confronted by innumerable compromises which present a very complex system of integration into his own internal nature and into the structures of his mind. All of these factors which enter into the interpretation of his life have given rise to the great national problem of mental health. It was pointed out that according to statistics, about ten million people are badly in need of psychiatric treatment; that there are over a half million people confined in various mental and other institutions, who are almost hopelessly involved in some type of mental aberration. More than fifty-five percent of the hospital beds of America are devoted to the use of such mental patients. If you closely examine the lives in the civilizations of other periods of history, you will see very clearly and very quickly that all this high rate of incidence in mental health, is strictly a product of the complexity of your present-day way of life. At no other time did any other civilization ever have the high incidence of mental aberration which is contained in your own present civilization.

If this mental problem is not very quickly solved, it is safe to assume that your great America, like many other civilizations, which for other reasons have gone down into the pages of oblivion in the historical accounts, must in some future day cease to exist. These factors which are involved in the innumerable pressures confronting the individual in his interpretation of life will, in a very short period of time, quickly undermine the social and moral structures of your great land.

We are not necessarily issuing this warning as an ultimatum. It is posed and presented to you purely as a very definite warning. In presenting the different facets of interpretation of spiritual law, order, and harmony in the different Shamballas, as your own earth comes somewhat under our care and guidance, and as we are to some degree responsible for your conditions, we are most anxious that these pressures shall be relieved.

How then, is this to be achieved? It cannot be done overnight nor can it be done strictly by enforcing another set of laws. This whole change of moral and social attitude and the underlying basic interpretation of moral structures as they exist in your country shall have to come, not from the government itself, but from within the individual concept as it is visualized within each individual. Each person must be educated by using the therapeutic methods which are available, so that at birth or infancy, he will properly be instituted in a correct relationship to his life as it must exist before him in the future days of his life upon the planet earth.

The reason for this condition in your country has been outlined previously. In the beginning of your nation, a group of individuals moralized and spiritualized certain dimensions of consciousness into the Constitution, and these men in themselves, were expressing a collective group of individualistic expressions; so that collectively, the fate of your future America will depend upon the individual expressions and in consequence, as to whether or not it shall become the leading and dominating spiritual power in its future evolutions.

As was previously pointed out to you, the earth is in itself going through an evolution. The atomic structures, the magnetic aura, or the magnetic structures of the universe about your earth as it progresses in its evolution, are also consequently changing. The people themselves must not be completely inflexible as they reincarnate into your dimension and consciousness. They must attain not only within their own dimension of consciousness the concepts of life, but must spring into renewed activity in this dimension; thus they can be properly nourished by such suitable environments.

The individual, in his evolutionary flight through the numerous dimensions of his life, should not at any time arrive at a state of consciousness which is less compatible than that which he had previously enjoyed in a previous reincarnation. This in itself would be contrary to the laws of cosmic evolution, for he would thus induce within himself more of the negative or karmic structures.

We are pointing out such corrective measures which will be of value in the future concepts of the people as they exist in your America, so that you can well be the pattern for future dimensions of concept as they exist in other countries upon the planet earth. These concepts must contain numerous interpretations of spiritual law, order, and harmony, which are not at the present time fully exercised in your own dimensions.

We have been largely pointing out to you the high rate of incidence in the various types of mental aberrations which are incurred in your civilization. However, these conditions are not necessarily confined in the channel of what we might call the insane, or those who are confined in mental institutions. The penal institutions of your country today, just as they have been in the past, are filled to overflowing with men and women who are in a very badly warped or distorted mental condition. We are not speaking of the small percentage of innocent victims who may have been impounded in these institutions, but only in the sense of the larger percentage of those who have been habitually inclined to the different criminal tendencies.

This subject is one of very vast and staggering proportions, indicating that each individual, in arriving at his own conclusions of criminal inclinations, has behind him a great deal of conflict within his own inner nature. Whether a man is a criminal or simply mentally aberrated means he has not only incurred a great deal of indisposition in his own transposition or interpretation of life, but that he has also incurred about him a great number of what are called obsessing entities. If the average citizen of your country could become momentarily clairvoyant so that he could see about him these numerous entities which have attached themselves to his magnetic aura, he might be so shocked that he would run screaming down the street. He might also, if he paused long enough to look about him, see that his fellow citizens were likewise entangled and enmeshed.

It goes without saying that practically every individual in his daily walk of life on earth as it exists today, is constantly under the dominion and the jurisdiction of one or a number of such spurious entities as he so interprets or regulates his thinking in his daily expression. The numerous vicissitudes of hate, anger, greed, and lust, whether they are sexual or other forms of passions, are in themselves somewhat cleverly contrived outbursts of his emotional nature which were inspired and induced by such spurious entities. Should the individual give way to any of these outbursts or interpretations of lust, hatred, greed, or avarice, he would not only be perverting his own true nature, but also encouraging one or a large group of such spurious entities to dominate and superimpose themselves further into his own spiritual consciousness.

You may very well ask the question: how it is that man has achieved any position which might be called civilized at the present moment, or how it is that he has come up through the numerous dimensions of time or historical evolutions on the earth, to have arrived at some status quo as he now exists upon the earth today? This in itself presents a very vast and complex interpretation regarding the nature and the evolution of spiritual laws, and their interpretation as they are going on about man.

We are not concerned with the short, individual life of any one person as he begins and leaves upon the earth any individualistic impressions of his own mind or interpretations. Thus we are saying that in itself the whole level of human consciousness, as it is expressed in the collective or enmassed interpretation of human relationship, is to a degree of incidence, the determining factor in the evolution of time.

In your world as you are becoming more and more conscious of the dominant factors of interpretation, you are seeing that there is—at the present time—a great struggle going on between the releasing of certain high spiritual concepts into your world and the suppression of these same spiritual concepts. There are many individuals on your earth today who have many very highly evolved spiritual concepts which are much in advance of the level of thinking or understanding of the ordinary individual of your time. They are, however, quite largely circumvented in the true expression of these spiritual concepts by the mere complexities of the expressions and their various interpretations.

In spiritual relationships as well as politics or other issues of life, the general public becomes somewhat apathetic if they cannot properly conceive a true and collective pattern of interpretation. They may well ask, that since these various and numerous differences existing in the spiritual and in the ecclesiastical orders are in such conflict and in such a strife in the dominion of their own interpretations, where then are these spiritual values so contained?

Man, therefore, stays away from the church or the lecture. Neither does he read the various and numerous books from which he might, if he possessed an analytical mind, get a great deal of value and virtue in extracting the truth from them. He may, and usually does, wind up with a general and a universal summary of all spiritual values and merely becomes an agnostic, saying, "Well, if I believe that Jesus can save me, then what is the use or necessity for pursuing some intensive course of spiritual interpretation?" Or he may say, "Well, if I try to do good to my fellow man, then surely I shall, in the future, find some sort of level or interpretation of spiritual values in any heaven at which I may arrive."

This type of thinking is dangerous, and is some-what of an opiate in the nature of a man's own personal concept. He must realize now, just as in the future, that he must put a great deal of emphasis and consideration into the course of his spiritual concept. He must properly evaluate experiences which come to him in the numerous dimensions of interpretation as he is convoluting in his many evolutions upon the various terrestrial planets. There is a great deal of conflicting literature available to the average individual, just as there are a great many contradictory spiritual interpretations. Consequently, the individual must possess some virtues of spiritual analysis and relationship in the interpretation of these various and numerous presentations of spiritual philosophies.

This condition is born out by the fact that there are about ten thousand different types of ecclesiastical or spiritual orders in existence in your America today. These could be very valuable adjuncts to the average individual in a comparative or an analytical sense, for he could derive much from the study and the correct interpretation of their expression.

It should be remembered by the individual, however, that he must be very analytical in his own concept; and that he must at no time lose sight of the fact that the true dimension of his own perspective and his own concepts, must come from within the higher reaches of his own individuality. He must be linked up with the dimension of the Superconsciousness and with the God force within him; otherwise, he may suffer a great deal of dereliction in the compounding of various elements which enter into his spiritual concept. He may become somewhat like a straw in the wind, which is constantly blown about when he finds the different facets and interpretations of life, as they exist in his own dimension and in his own time.

While a great deal of this vacillation is true of the average individual in his lower elemental orders, yet at some time he must begin to conclude a certain strength and a certain purpose in the course of his own personal evolution. He must begin to realize that he is the dominant factor in this evolution and that he himself must start to choose the numerous virtues, and reject the negative expressions of life which are compounded and in which he finds himself. He must, at all times, remain constant in the expression of a great deal of moral strength and in the judicial selection of these numerous virtues, that they may be so related and so compounded within his own concept that they will integrate him into a dimension wherein he is a being of organized consciousness and conception.

I might point out that there are numerous deceptions and subterfuges in the many interpretations and concepts of life, and that people sometimes very inadvertently read into such concepts, or in their evaluations, some preconceived and erroneous notion which was superimposed in some unrelative dimension of life. We are stressing the importance of realizing the obsessive nature of the various dimensions of spiritual contact in which man is evolving, for these conditions have been largely neglected and disregarded. In fact, they have been misconstrued as witchcraft or sorcery. In separating himself from this dimension of concept, man has incurred into his own consciousness a great deal of harm and error, which otherwise could have been largely averted.

The average individual in the numerous civilizations in the planet earth today, has neglected to properly place the concept of obsessions and the possibilities of the invasion of these spiritual dimensions into his consciousness. As a result, he is so dominated by obsessing or possessing entities that he can very well become the sad victim of some of these entities.

The old adage that "forewarned is forearmed" is very useful here, and should be used in the concept of the average individual, for by knowing of the existence of, and the way in which the different spiritualistic entities can enter into his dominion or consciousness, he can properly circumvent such incursions and intrusions into his own concepts. Man has a Superconscious Mind wherein is contained all the elements of self-preservation and he is also properly linked up with other preservative elements in the dimensions of spiritual consciousness. He will thus automatically, as you might say, immunize himself to a large degree, against these invasive and possessive forces from the lower orders of spiritual consciousness. Here we are showing you—just as we hope these lines will reach the general public—the results of the malpractice of eliminating spiritual values and interpretations from the way of life, since all individuals can incur numerous types of obsessions.

The actual facts are, that there is not a single individual upon the earth today who is not in some way, and has not been at some time, induced or coerced by some spiritual elements or infractions of these spiritual interpretations which come from various entities and from subastral dimensions. Even the more highly developed intellects, by the element of ignorance, are, to a large degree, unable properly to insulate themselves against the intrusions and invasions of these elemental expressions from subastral entities. In examining the histories and the philosophies of the world, the student may become aware that there was a great deal of knowledge concerning these spiritual concepts in the numerous interpretations, whether they related to pure ecclesiastical or spiritual concepts, or as to whether they were so contained in the numerous more materialistic philosophies.

At my time, many of my own countrymen expressed within these philosophies, elements of understanding, which we at that time, called demons or obsessive spirits. The gods themselves, as they were contained in the understanding of the Pantheon, and as we, at that time more or less contained them in the votive or ecclesiastic concepts, were destructive demons in themselves; and then, as now, man was more or less subject to the influences of demonized possessions, just as he was subject to the higher and more spiritual infiltrations of consciousness.

Throughout the hundreds of years following the Reformation, the great Holy Roman Empire acknowledged in very numerous concessions, as they burned people at the stake, that there was indeed a great deal of witchery and sorcery in existence. This church at that time, just as they and other denominations do today, included in the curricular education of the future priests, clergymen, and ministers, concepts which can properly be called exorcisms.

The last rites of a Catholic priest to a dying man are based primarily upon the concept that the man must be given safe conduct through certain lower orders of hellish entities into some higher concept. The purgatory of Catholic ritualism is itself a direct admission of a great number of these spurious negative entities and their obsession and possession of people. Therefore, at no time in the pages of history, can we ever separate man in his consciousness from the elements of spiritual influences, unless it is in the pages of your own American history.

The very practitioners who call themselves psychiatrists, who are so vitally concerned with the future destinies of their patients and hold within their hands the very life substance of these patients, ignore and completely exclude some of the factors which relate the individual to his spiritual dimensions of consciousness. These concepts within the patient's mind are so very badly maligned and warped that he may fall victim of the plagues and hordes of infesting spirits which may, at that moment, be infiltrating into his consciousness.

I might point out that until the consciousness or the level of concept of the practitioner or the man of medicine or psychiatry, as he exists today, is brought up to the understanding whereby he can properly introduce into the dominion of his practice, the proper elements and knowledge of spiritual laws in the true domain of their relationship to the individual patient (and he must not misconstrue the primitive expressions of sorcery or witchcraft in the primitive tribes of people as they existed in the past or in the present time of your earth age), he cannot expect to obtain the desired healings and corrections.

The savage in the jungle, in practicing his various medicine rituals as he dances about the gods or demons of his own conception, is, in his own way, giving a very elemental interpretation of these spiritual principles. This ritual may do a great deal of good to the savage who is subjected to the fears of superstition and coercion of this type of interpretation. However, this is very far removed from what is called a very factual, wise, and logical interpretation of practice of a much higher concept.

The development of this concept in itself, just as it would be in any other field of medicine, is one which will involve many years of experimentation in the minds of the individuals who are inclined to pursue these fields of investigation. They must, by the reason of their own experience, incur the principles of wisdom and the relationship of those spiritual concepts into their own practice. These concepts could not be contained in so many pages or in so many words; instead they must be in themselves a pure product and an evolution of time and the age in which man is living at that time.

The practice of medicine and the development of antibiotic drugs and the various other constituents in medical practices, as they exist today, have been the development and the evolution which have involved a great number of years. In the future, the development of proper values of that which might be called exorcism or the casting out of evil obsessions will come into general usage and practice; and will be the greatest contributing factor in dispersing the evils of spiritual neglect, which have relegated such large masses of people to the threshold of insanity, and even beyond. Thus it will be that great masses of humanity will be saved the unnecessary reincarnations and devastations of being plunged into the concepts of abysmal ignorance as they exist in the lower world orders of obsessing entities, which are the derivatives of such misunderstandings and malpractices.

To point out further the innumerable types of obsessions or possessions, as they enter into the evaluations of the concepts and interpretations of your daily life, I could, as was done by Hippocrates, lead you through the remaining sections of this vast center wherein he teaches, and show you the different obsessive natures of idea thought-forms or the actual entities themselves. For instance, here we see those who have been so obsessed by sex during their earth life, that their thought-created obsessions will assume the proportion of sex organs to such a gigantic extent that the individual will be completely engulfed by— or changed into—a representation of a sexual organ. The whole concept of living with the idea of sex, as it is developed in many individuals on earth today, does develop them along the lines whereby they become somewhat of a spiritual concept of an overdeveloped sexual organ.

The man or woman who does nothing but pursue the almighty dollar (and this in itself, has a tremendous repercussion in the changing of the individual's spiritual contour) may become so warped and distorted that he loses all semblance or form of an individual. Such individuals have, to a large degree, compounded in their psychic bodies the intelligences —if I can call them such—or the facets of life which are contained in the money symbols and in the contents of the exchange systems of the dimension in which they are living. These things are not in a spiritual sense at all relative and are not contained in the spiritual transition of the individual. These concepts must be rectified and eliminated; and therefore the individual must return to some suitable dimension which is elemental in nature and must restart his evolution to reconstruct his psychic body.

The whole idea supporting reincarnation (and the only true answer to life) is the evaluation of man's evolution into the higher consciousness of life. The contents of one's psychic body, as he is individually so constituted at this time, will not remain with him into what we call the eternities or the vistas of the future.

The psychic body, just as does all things, changes in its evolution; and the truths in numerous reincarnations are the infractions impounded into the psychic body. Such wave forms or vortexes are undergoing a spiritual evolution to such an extent that they become refined and attain a higher dimensional infusion so as to more properly relate themselves to the true spiritual concepts, as it is evaluated by the portrayal of the Life Cycle as it was conceived in the individual from the Mind of God. This in itself is the true answer to the purpose and destiny of man. He should never be confused by false doctrines which stem purely from the various complexes of certain individuals who do not properly understand the orders of law and harmony and frequency relationships.

The practitioner, teacher, or clergyman may quite easily circumvent the true spiritual evolution of a large group of individuals in his misunderstanding and interpretation. There is a good deal of altar worship and such orthodox conceptions in existence today, which must be completely rectified and eliminated in the future evolutions of the individual's mind, and may be at the time, constituting elements which are somewhat stabilizing in his own existence. Yet they may very well become, as I have said, an opiate in his future translation, wherein he believes that these things in themselves are virtues of his own salvation, as it has been repeatedly pointed out. The virtue of salvation is only contained in evolution, and the evolution of the individual must, as it does by necessity, refract and infract into itself all of the dimensions of God's own Infinite Mind and Purpose. These elements cannot be properly compounded or impounded into his nature without the value of the emotional experience as he inscribes these things unto himself.

This is the necessary and ultimate purpose of evolution. The idea of evolution, or reincarnation as it is called, is subject to a wide degree of variation and interpretation, as it is conceived by the individual today on the earth plane. We have stated in previous transmissions that the average individual will very frequently reincarnate or revolve about a certain terrestrial dimension of understanding; and in the concept of the terrestrial natures and understandings of these concepts, he continually re-relates himself in an outward way by reincarnating as a physical being into such a terrestrial dimension.

We do not, in any sense of the word, wish to be misconstrued as to our stand upon this purpose, for were we misunderstood, the consequence would be illogical. However, the average individual, in his elemental orders of understanding, is very illogical in himself. He could if he contained some small grain of truth, or if he could see his own purpose of life, eliminate many of these evolutions which would be quite unnecessary to him if he properly understood the values of life.

By the same token, many of the small children who are coming into the world today could be taught properly the spiritual evolution so that each child, too, could be saved many thousands of years and countless impingements of karmic error into consciousness, which must be rectified later. Ignorance itself breeds ignorance, and the consequence of ignorance must always be individually worked out by the person who has so incurred the ignorance into his own consciousness.

If the average child coming into the world today was taught that he was merely the product of spiritual evolution, and that he existed only in this place of consciousness for certain definite purposes, that he must be very careful to impound only elements of spiritual wisdom and virtue in his future translations of life; he would very quickly arrive at a point where he would be saved the numerous reincarnations. He might also be saved from becoming one of the inmates of your mental or penal institutions.

The proper understanding of evolution or reincarnation, will factually interrelate every human concept as it exists upon the earth today. Every individual, in the diagnosis of his material or spiritual status quo, can be properly diagnosed into being further re-educated and reorientated into the concepts of life. The existence of error in any individual's life, means only that there has been some dereliction of spiritual principle in his evolution. It means that he has merely been ignorant or unconscious of the spiritual interpretations, or even far worse, he may have known something of them and still indulged in some dereliction. This in itself has a much greater degree of impact into his own nature.

So, dear brothers and sisters, do not misconstrue or listen to the false words of those who are about you, in the various interpretations of spiritual law as they relate to you in your own personal evolution. Reincarnation or evolution, as has been so previously explained, will relate each individual into his own concept in his proper sequence and order. He comes into the world by way of the womb at the moment of conception. He does not reincarnate into any living soul; or, if he so reincarnates into a living soul, he is merely possessing or obsessing the living soul by attaching himself to its magnetic aura.

There is only one way in which a person can reincarnate into this world, and that is through the proper relationship of the law of frequency and harmonic relationships. The individual, in his spiritual domain wherever he so resides, contains within the structure and elements of the psychic body, such concepts as will vibrate in such harmonic conclusion that he will be automatically drawn into the channel of birth where he is conceived into the womb, and will emerge as a human being. The whole superstructure, or as he is overshadowed, will be within the dominion of the spiritual concepts which are contained in the individual's psychic body. The concepts of one's psychic body are not contained within the concepts of any other individual, unless some other individual becomes possessive or obsessive, and attaches himself into the magnetic aura of the individual.

We must never at any time, misconstrue or misinterpret what is properly called reincarnation or karma. Karma is itself only a consequence, or the result of wrong interpretation, or thinking, or execution, of our interpretation of principle. If the thinking is wrong, the error must and can be visualized by the individual in the future spiritual consciousness as something which retards him. He sees within his own self, such defects of consciousness as have been termed mental or spiritual blocks. He will thus say to himself, "I must remove these blocks which are impeding my progress."

Man will thus seek a level of interpretation where these blocks were incurred, and he will try in some way to remove them in some other integration of concept, which will be at such proper position of polarity that it will cancel out these blocks or impingements of error and interpolation in his consciousness, if the proper relationship of harmonic structure is brought into being at the proper moment in his evolution.

These numerous blocks or vortexes can thus very quickly and properly be removed from man's consciousness. Just as the housewife who irons the various pieces of clothing of her family by pushing the hot iron upon the cloth, so the individual places the Light of Truth and shines it directly into the block as it is contained in the psychic body. He cannot do this at the time in which it is incurred; instead, it must be done at such proper time and in such proper relationship of harmonic law and order, so that this Light of Truth, or the Christ Light of his own consciousness, can eliminate and rectify this mental obstruction.

The average individual must also be made to realize that there can be a great deal of intercession to help and aid him in working out these various spiritual interpretations in his own life, if he so properly conceives the Intercessors, and can call upon them or bring them into focus in a proper relationship, in the removal of these obstructions in his own evolution. As was pointed out, there are great levels of spiritual interpretation in the domains or, shall I say, in the spiritual planets such as the Shamballas, wherein reside countless millions of individual concepts or polarized individuals who can, and very often do, respond to the call of the individual in lower dimensions to aid and abet him in his evolution and soul flight. However, it must be borne in mind at all times, that it is not the Christ, but will be so interpreted in other concepts as the Christ Consciousness of the individual, which comes from his own Superconsciousness.

The various types of intercession or aid to the individual, comes from such spiritual levels which would be in direct harmonic relationship to his own life. The Intercessors will not in themselves as individuals, reach down, as you might say, through a hole in a cloud and take the individual by the scruff of his coat and snatch him from some abysmal pit of clay where he has plunged himself. Instead, these higher dimensional spiritual forces will refer certain elements of their own consciousness in the proper orders of spiritual or harmonic relationships into the individual's consciousness. He will thus be able, in his future evolutions, to begin to impound, or, shall I say, to digest or to integrate these high orders of spiritual rays or Light of Truth, into his consciousness. He will thus automatically lift his feet from the pit of clay where he has plunged himself.

The person who is indulging himself in the fallacious interpretation of intercession must know that intercession cannot come, as I have just pointed out, from some great spiritual hand which will snatch him from oblivion. Intercession comes only through the individual concept as man so relates himself to spiritual concepts in the evolution and in the translation of his own ideals and moral values. He must do all these things by himself. The general end result is that he must be individualized as he is going through the various emotional values of impounding these spiritual concepts within his own nature. Just as the child learns not to touch the flame of a candle, so the individual in the future learns not to touch any elements which, in themselves, are spurious or negative in the conclusions of his own concepts; and that he will thus learn, in his future evolutions in flights into the higher spiritual dimensions, to properly integrate the higher facets of truth into his own consciousness.

This, my dear ones, is your intercession, your own personal salvation. There stands by you, and ready at all times, a great multitude of more highly evolved and developed souls from the higher dimensions who will, shall I say, shine the rays of their own wisdom and knowledge into your own consciousness. As to how you use these rays of Truth or Light depends entirely on yourself, and you may or may not be conscious that such things can exist. A positive consciousness is quite often very conducive or inductive to attuning a person to a higher spiritual dimension, even momentarily, so that such rays of Light and

Truth can shine into his consciousness or into his subconsciousness.

Powerful radiant energies which stem from the great vortex itself are contained in the higher dimensions. They also infuse and infiltrate into some of the intercessions of man's dimensional relationships. However, it is always the concepts of the individual himself, for he must manifest and exercise this consciousness in his daily life. If man deviates, even momentarily, from the consciousness of this vast spiritual dimension of consciousness from which he has come, and to which he must return, he separates himself from the most positive attributes of this spiritual consciousness. Thus he must, in consequence, become negative and so subjects himself to the great seas of spiritual negation which also exist in direct polarity or contrast to the positive spheres of spiritual consciousness.

In coming into the elements of this negation, man must therefore subject himself to the numerous multitudes of entities or individual expressions of these negative energies. These negative energies are just as real as the energies which stem from the vast central vortex; but they are all energies which will further lead the individual astray in his own purpose and intent from his true course of evolution.

However, dear ones, this subject is in itself, vast. I could go on for many hours and continually enlarge the concept of the spiritual truth into your consciousness; but I am limited somewhat by the physical strength of the channel, so that for the time being, may I remain your true friend and brother in spirit,

— Apollonius of Tyana

CHAPTER 83

My dear brothers and sisters, I am most happy to renew our exploration again into this section of Parhelion. For personal identity, I am Hippocrates, one of the teachers here, who gave a previous transmission.

The preceding transmission, was a general discussion of elemental factors in your civilization and the summary of reincarnation by my very worthy brother, Apollonius of Tyana, who generalized somewhat on the various aspects of life and civilization and personal evolution.

We can now resume somewhat more of a direct exploration here into another of these sections, which is devoted to the general practice and understanding of psychiatry and medicine in various terrestrial and astral dimensions.

In our previous visit, you were taken to the section which was somewhat devoted to teaching various students the results of obsession and possession of evil entities or thought-form bodies; and you and sister were made quite nauseated by the sight of these numerous squirming eel-like or leech-like creatures which had infested and attached themselves onto the psychic bodies and structures of some unfortunate beings. You saw also, the result of malformation of the psychic bodies, in which the various persons twisted and distorted themselves by perversions of different concepts, such as sex, or money, or other materialistic values. This subject is also one which is quite vast; and while we have somewhat generalized in presenting some of these things to you, you must also realize that we could continue for many hours in the same general line of exploration and discussion. However, at this moment, we shall go to a section which is related more directly at the present time, to the practice of medicine on the earth, as it is in its present form.

May I first say, that the physician who very conscientiously applies himself to his practice, and if he is altruistically inclined or motivated in his sole interest of rehabilitating or reconstituting the physical body, is to be complimented. Medical science as it exists today has made tremendous and advanced strides, especially in the last fifty or hundred years.

However, it is customary at your time to give a great deal of wrong and false emphasis on a credence as to the advanced state of your medical science. There is also too much of the principle of specialization in the general practice of medicine. A doctor may very often, in his own specialized form or expression of medicine, overlook some very pertinent and vital defect in the constitution of a human being, which is entirely unrelated to the symptom itself. For example, we know that a headache, or even eyestrain, may sometimes be caused by the displacement of bones in the longitudinal arch of the foot or by the falling of muscular tones, as they are compounded in the ligaments and muscular tendons of the calf of the leg.

It is common knowledge that any of the symptoms of illness which are distressing the human body, very often occur and recur at different points of the body, which are quite remote from their original cause. The nervous system of the human being is one which is quite capable of producing, in somewhat of a harmonic fashion, a series or a combination of impulses which are painful in nature in some sympathetic region which is not the region or original inception of pain or distress. I am purposely avoiding the nomenclature of the physician, as he so contains himself in the expression of his medical science, for the obvious reasons that these terms would somewhat confuse the general reader, to whom this book is dedicated.

Now that we have arrived here at this particular section, as you look about you, you will be amazed at the vast size of this gallery or section into which you are just entering. Here is a factual cross section, not only of the terrestrial dimension in the practice of medicine, in which you will see actual operating rooms and hospital wards and operations just as they would be on the earth, but you may also see some operating rooms or wards as they exist in other terrestrial dimensions.

These things are brought into realization for the student in the comparative values and equations in his own personal relationship, as he is being so educated or taught in the evolution of medicine as it will, quite by necessity, resolve itself into future expressions of time. The medicine which you practice today will be quite as remote and as obsolete and outmoded in a hundred years from now, as the medicine of a hundred years ago is outmoded in your time and day.

However, do not, as I have said, take too much of a stamp of false credence or pride, that you have conceived or contrived a medical science which has been and which is in existence for the first time on the face of the planet earth; or that you have achieved some relationship in this science which is superior to all time. It is quite true that there is a general course of extreme specialization and mechanization in the field of medicine, which is unique in your time and dimension. However, it must be born in mind that medical practice, as it existed in other civilizations, was quite as relative and quite as effectual in its own interpretation, as is yours in your present day and in your present world.

Among the ancient Toltecs and Aztecs of Central and South America and in such places as China and Egypt, surgeons performed operations on the brain which were known as trephining; and they performed other such vivisections or dissections of the human anatomy. This was done without the commonly known instruments of anesthesia, as you know or conceive of them in your time and dimension. The anesthesia which was used at that time was more of a trance state. In some instances, the individual was actually transported from his physical body and held in a suspended state in an astral world while the operation was performed upon the body. The individual was then later replaced in his body, and he then proceeded in the healing process and was soon able to function in a very normal way.

Other methods of anesthesia consisted of something more of a hypcognic or hypnotic nature, produced from the fumes of various herbs whose drugs were liberated in the process of combustion. As the patient inhaled these fumes, he became completely anesthetized and was therefore unaware that anything was being done to his body. These processes are all quite similar to one basic aspect of relationship: it merely temporarily severs the patient from the conscious realization of the screen of his life, as it is known by his objective or reasoning consciousness.

The suspension of relationship is in the frontal lobes of the brain, which relates man to the reasoning faculties of his nature. Do not assume, however,

811

that these reasoning factors are contained in the brain. The brain itself, is only the outward artifice of a very cleverly contrived mechanism of atomic structures, which are related in themselves to the psychic body from whence the dimension of concept springs in the daily lifetime of the individual.

The brain contains nothing which is generic in its nature; nor does it manufacture, in itself, any of the compounded complexities of nerve impulses which are constantly stemming into the extremities of the human body. These, in themselves, are likewise products of the contents of the psychic body in the vibrationary nature, which relate themselves to the universal and cosmic source of all energy.

The physician of the earth today, takes pride in feeling that he is somewhat responsible for extending the span of human life. While this is quite true in some relative aspects, we must compare the statistics which state that man lives ten or twelve years longer than he did at some comparatively recent time. We must take these statistics on the analysis from which they were so compounded; they could be quite wrongfully slanted in a false interpretation. The great plagues of the past, such as the bubonic, or the epidemics of flu, smallpox, and various other types of diseases which decimated whole populations, have now vanished; but there have been other decimators of human population which are rapidly taking their place; these lie within the dimension of that which is called mental illness.

The mental illnesses in themselves are twofold in their destructive nature. An individual cannot be immunized against a mental illness, except through the induction of spiritual principles within his consciousness. This cannot be done with a needle, or with any other manufactured type of vaccine which might be contained and manufactured from a test tube in a laboratory.

The two-fold nature and propensities of mental illnesses not only manifest themselves into the sphere of the consciousness of the individual in his mental faculties, but may in future generations, and in different ways, also remanifest themselves into his physical structures. Simply because a person is not incarcerated in a mental institution, and classified as having some paranoiac or repressive complex, does not mean that he is not mentally ill. Most of the patients who are lying in hospital beds and those who are somewhat partially incapacitated in their daily way of life, due to various aches and pains which are manifest in different conditions and concepts, are, in themselves, all directly related to the mental processes of the faculties of the human individual.

It is a general consensus of opinion among the physicians, surgeons, and psychiatrists in the world today, that at least 90% of those illnesses do stem from the mental processes of the individual; and he is linked to the negative aspects of life so that he becomes inductive in his relationship to the various types of physical illnesses in his body. So now we are beginning to understand the two-fold nature of any type of mental illness which can be properly called a negative state of consciousness.

Just as in an obsessive or a possessive state of consciousness, these mental illnesses (and I shall call them psychic aberrations), in consequence, can make an individual become partially or wholly insane in some mental way, so that his physical deficiencies can be classified roughly in two dimensions. The thought-form bodies, incurred in this possessive way, may warp and largely destroy the mental concepts so that these bodies can be generated within the consciousness of the individual to such an extent that they can completely obsess his physical body. It is common knowledge that in hypnosis, a person can be autosuggestively induced into such a state that he will walk the rest of his life with a limp, although there will be nothing wrong with his leg.

A person as a child might incur some small accident which, in the sphere of the imagination, may create such a horror of the accident, that it could induce such a strong autosuggestive thought pattern, that the accident may permanently maim or cripple the individual for the rest of his life, even though the injury may have healed within a few months' time after its inception; and the body was, in consequence, just as whole and as functional as it ever was. However, the person by that time would have induced this strong thought pattern into his relationship so that he would go through life with this very strongly induced physical malformation which did not actually exist.

Many of the leaders of some of the spiritual cults or expressions in life, who have become noted as spiritual healers, have somewhat capitalized upon this idea of liberation of self through the autosuggestive processes of man's nature. In the temples or churches, these so-called and purported spiritual healers cry unto the persons that they are healed and the persons believe they are healed. They immediately cast aside and disengage themselves from this strong adhesive thought pattern, and suddenly come into the realization that there was nothing actually wrong with them. So they toss their crutches, or their braces, or their supports into the corner with the others and walk from the temple. Thus they cry that these healers are indeed great servants of God, for they have been healed; whereas they could have done the same thing for themselves many years ago and thus saved a great deal of time, trouble, and expense.

If you look about you in the institutions and in the highways and byways of your time and place, you will see many persons either in hospital beds, or partially or wholly incapacitated in their daily lives from these very strongly superimposed thought structures. Indeed it is sometimes very difficult for these people to liberate themselves. Some of these individuals are very masochistic in their nature, and are continually punishing themselves for their faults and misplaced conceptions which have given rise to great structures of guilt complexes. They are punishing themselves for believing themselves to be inadequate, or believing they have expressed some great sin into their concepts of life.

In India, there is a fraction of the population, called in their own concept, the Jains. Jainism is an extrusion of one of the concepts of Buddhism, as it is brought down through Vishnu, and into the lower caste orders of the different systems of Buddhism as they exist in India. These Jainists constantly punish themselves by running large needles through their cheeks, or they may variously impale themselves in different portions of their anatomy; or they may lie upon spiked beds to further torture themselves in almost fantastic proportions which are almost beyond the concept of your imagination.

And yet you, in your own civilized world, see people who are actually doing the very same thing in their daily walk of life. There is no difference in the attitude or mentality of the individual, for they are so consciously related that they express themselves in this conscious relationship in this self-inflicted masochism.

815

As every doctor knows, there are many patients in his experience who have come to him with nothing wrong with them physically, except that they have very strongly induced thought patterns which are so inducted in their nature, that they have actually made the individuals ill, and rendered them, as a consequence of this self-induced illness, wholly or partially incapacitated.

The very simple and common ailment of headache, as it is so expressed in the general run of human beings as they exist about you in your own dimension, is in itself purely a product of hypertension. Incidentally, I might mention this is one of the ills of the human race today which is literally killing people by the thousands every year. Hypertension is purely a byproduct of what Freud called the libido or drive; the tension of the times in which you are living. As was pointed out by Apollonius, the various pressures are induced, not only by governmental systems, but by the social and religious structures which exist around you, as you, in your various ways, are contriving to arrive at certain compensations and evaluations in these pressures.

Every doctor knows that each patient coming to him in his practice, has symptoms which, in themselves, may indicate certain presupposed malformations or functions of the body; yet in a final diagnosis, there may be a whole host of other inductive conditions which have contrived to induce this condition into the human body. And as a consequence, every physician is confronted with a great deal of experimentation.

The age of specialization in which you now live, is in itself one which is also quite subject to a great deal of error. The physician who is specializing in some section of the anatomy may, in some presupposed symptom as it appears in the body, so classify or wrongly relegate this symptom into something which may in a future day, cause a great deal of harm and frustration in the mind and body of the patient. Here again it would be a very valuable adjunct to the physician if he could be sufficiently clairvoyant just as some practitioners have been, both in medicine and in science and in the pure fields of ecclesiastics, and could peer into the body of the patient in such an X-ray fashion as to properly place the illnesses and their corrective therapies in his own mind.

That this has been done in your time and dimension, has been very properly demonstrated by such men as Dr. Peebles, and by another man known as Edgar Cayce, who lived at Virginia Beach. The actual case histories of this latter individual are completely and thoroughly substantiated and are a matter of medical record.

Going back a little further to the time of Jesus who performed the same kind of miracles in corrective and therapeutic medicine by relieving many individuals of various painful diseases; he, too, could peer into the anatomy of the human being and properly see there the exact causation of such a diseased condition. As has been pointed out, these diseased conditions, in themselves, were not necessarily something which was induced at the time of the appearance of the disease in the individual when he so lived on the earth at that time. It could have been, and was quite often the case, that the condition was the result of a great psychic impact into the individual's nature and into a life which he had previously lived at some other place and time.

The direct result of the appearance of any physical condition or malformation in the human body must always be properly evaluated first, as it is wrong alignment in some respect to the patient's own attitude or aspect of life. Because these dimensional factors, or relationships, or inceptions in his spiritual nature have not been properly interjected, he has been unable to perform as a natural, normal human being. The inflow of Infinite Energy, as it is expressed in different dimensional relationships into the individual in one, or a number, of these dimensional expressions, has somehow been misaligned; or the individual has been temporarily tuned out from the true conscious purpose of his spiritual life.

In going down this great corridor, which is devoted to the teaching of these medical practices in the different terrestrial and astral dimensions, just as in the various operating rooms and hospitals of the numerous places of your own terrestrial world, you will see replicas of these many instrumentations and their usage as they are demonstrated by the teachers. As the student progresses along the line of integrating the factors of evolution in medical science, he will thus, in consequence, be able to reincarnate into some dimension of expression where he will be able to reproduce very factually, a higher concept of the practice of medicine into that future day and time.

The element of human progress, in the evolution or the mental level of any civilization, as it has been so demonstrated or impounded in any historical empire or civilization, whether it existed upon your planet or upon any of the other numerous planets, has always been directly the byproduct of evolution of individuals, who have learned, or contrived, or fashioned some philosophical or scientific aspect of their lives in a higher spiritual realm. And so in reincarnating and beginning to develop this spiritual science, in a comparatively lower level, they have thus been able to serve mankind and to help lead them just a little farther along the line of their own personal evolution.

Here we do not confine evolution into the pure individual concept, but rather into the collective level of civilization as it exists as a whole. As you witnessed during the period of Reformation, the intellectual level of people was led into a freer and a higher state of expression, not necessarily by one individual or one field of endeavor, but it was propagated and inspired and further aided and abetted by various and numerous persons in different fields of endeavor. So in the overall evaluation of that period, it can be said that man was indeed led into the furtherance and betterment of his own spiritual self, and into following a genuine purpose and pattern of evolution of consciousness.

Your present day expresses a certain level of consciousness, which is somewhat of a mechanized way of life. You have thus contrived around you, such a tremendous fabrication and superstructure of mechanical contrivances, that your whole world has thus become something which reminds us of a great boiler factory, where there is a great deal of sawing and pounding and hammering going on at all times. As a result, the din and noise, and the confusion itself, is something which would distract even a more complacent person into fleeing to some remote section of the planet.

The great highways which link your cities become veritable slaughterhouses, in which you yearly sacrifice many thousands of people in your mad haste to get somewhere; and when you get there, you very often just sit or lie around and do nothing at all. There is very often a great lack of cohesion and reason in the many things which human beings do upon their planet at this particular time. However, this has somewhat been the case with all evolutions of mankind, inasmuch as they do not relate themselves with the more highly evolved principles of their spiritual nature.

Mankind, living on the earth today, is purely in the elemental stages. Do not pride yourselves that your civilization is too high or advanced in its concept. As we have said, this too, is a principle of relativity, and as you leave your terrestrial dimensions, you will be somewhat surprised to know, just as we do, that the terrestrial planet of the earth is one of the very basic, and first, and elemental planes of understanding of man and his relationship to his higher God-self and his true nature.

We here, just as myself, so very earnestly stress and lay the strongest emphasis upon compounding the expressions within your daily lives as they exist about you. The more advanced spiritual concepts relate man to his true spiritual self, for man is truly a spiritual being, even though he lives in a terrestrial dimension, which you say is composed of mass; and this, too, is only a product of concept. Man, in his higher Superconsciousness, along with the combining elements which the Infinite God has so contrived and conceived as the dimensions of mass into his consciousness of thinking, would in his evolution, be given individuality and the purpose of his conception.

In the future day of medicine, the doctor who will live on the terrestrial planet one hundred years from now, may very well be a doctor who will be somewhat similar to the doctor of the past, as in the ancient Egyptian science of medicine, as it was practiced during the time of Osiris.

People in that day and age were very often relieved of conditions which the modern surgeon of today would find almost, if not totally, incurable. The patient was first separated from his physical body in what has sometimes been called a trance, or an astral state. With the patient hanging thus suspended, the physician or practitioner or whatever you would call him, was able, with the help of practitioners and doctors from the higher dimensions, to interject such therapy into the temporarily unconscious body, that whatever illness was present was immediately arrested. This was done without instruments and without dismemberment of the body in any way. There are, of course, many variations of this more highly evolved and developed technique.

Spiritual healing in its pure sense, as was practiced by Jesus, meant that the patient, in his complete and abject faith in approaching the Master Avatar, was completely lifted from the plane of consciousness in which he was living and reinstated into another spiritual plane, or dimension, in the true concept of his mind. Thus the body was actually instantaneously following the spiritual concept, or the dimension in which the nature of the individual had been placed. An instantaneous corrective therapy was thus instituted in the body of the individual. This in itself is purely a highly developed principle of concept, and one into which every individual in his future evolution will develop, as he progresses according to the normal order and relationship or law of evolution. He will arrive at a place in his dimension where he will know how to do this, not only for others, but for himself also.

As a direct consequence of this much more highly developed nature and in the compounding of the spiritual virtues which he finds in the dimension in which he now is, man will, in consequence, not incur the various infractions of negative presuppositions into his nature. Nor will he suffer from the physical illnesses which are the byproducts of negativity, mis-understanding, fear, and ignorance; for these con-ditions are purely produced within the realm and dimension of fear, ignorance, superstition, and mal-practice of any spiritual virtues which may be con-tained in the individual's consciousness.

In the future day, the weapons and guns of war and the battleships and the various impedimenta of the armies and navies which you so frantically construct (since you believe in a defense against destructive powers) shall be melted down into the plowshares to turn over the fertile earth as you have so familiarly termed it.

Your instruments, your scalpels, your various con-trivances which are used for anesthesia, and many of the artifacts of present medical science, shall likewise be relegated to the dump heap; and these, too, shall be melted down into more useful instrumentation for the future world. The patient of tomorrow will be, indeed, a much more fortunate individual.

The masses of humans who are striving in the dimension of terrestrial expression as they are on the earth today, so steeped in the fear of ignorance and superstition in the age and time in which they live, are so warped and contorted in their expression and way of life, that these things do seem to us here to pose a problem of tremendous scope; and they can-not be alleviated in any one immediate age or in one immediate dimension.

The individuals as they express themselves indi-vidually, in the concept of your time and in your place, must by necessity relieve themselves of such karma as they have incurred in the initiative factors of negative thinking in the presuppositions of the civilization instituted about them; and men must in consequence ascend into the higher dimensions which are above them. If individuals do not do so, then they must expect to revert to the universal cosmos, sometimes referred to as space. They will revert back into the sea of cosmic energy, from whence God so contrived and fashioned them as individual concepts of His own being.

The ultimate and conclusive principles of man's evolutions cannot, and will not, be presented to you in this book or in any other book which might lead to dimensions which are beyond the finite concept of your own dimension at this time. You will, by necessity and for the wisdom of the purpose contained therein, be given only such fractions as are relative to your own individual evolution and progress.

The infinity of God's own nature, and the dimensions in which God is so expressed and realized, are indeed something which would not only stagger but confound and confuse you. Even though we ourselves have evolved into a dimension where we become more introspective, as well as retrospective, we too might, if we looked beyond the horizon of our spiritual dimension, become somewhat confused, just as would you. So we must not at any time, strive or stress or place false emphasis onto such values which we are not properly able to conceive or interweave into our own personal progression or evolution. Nor should we try to compound such infractions or portions of other individual concepts into our own structure, unless they too can be factually integrated as they may become something of relative consequence to us.

The expression of the "blind leading the blind" is one which is a very factual reality in the earth about you today. There are many persons who are going about in their daily lives trying to inflict their various philosophies, or facets, or interpretations of life upon their fellow men, even though they themselves very often do not understand the nature of these principles, or the true relationship of these principles within themselves.

Primarily, we might say that these extrusions of mentality from one man to another are not born strictly from a more humanitarian concept of nature. The individual who is striving to impress another individual as to his own concept or his own personal attainment or his mental or spiritual stature is doing so more directly from some of the more inductive processes which are called guilt complexes. He may, in the consciousness and in the fear and the superstition and the unrelative sequence of factors in his own concept, be so motivated that he will try to placate his own consciousness by interjecting what he thinks is right upon the consciousness of some other individual.

What is of the most value and of the greatest importance to the individual, lies within the realm and dimension of his own consciousness. We would stress most emphatically the concept, as it was expounded by Jesus, that if you seek for the Kingdom of Heaven which is within, all things shall be added unto you. This is factually a concept which will be of the greatest value to you. If you so believe and so conceive, then the principles of the truths which may arise from the analytical processes of the higher nature within yourself, can aid and help you in contriving a philosophy which will be inductive in its nature to your higher self.

As has been pointed out and so emphatically stressed, the greatest principles of truth which have been of the greatest value to the progress of human evolution, have not come from without, or the exteriors, or the superficialities of man's nature, in the translation of life about him. Instead, they have, and must, come from within man himself. In man's periods of meditation or cognition of his own Superconsciousness or of the values of spiritual dimensions which he may not be able to classify, yet in the inspirational values which are contained in these contacts, he has brought in a conclusive relationship, some philosophy or science into his own dimension. He may even be so motivated in these concepts that he may accidentally reproduce them. One of the antibiotic drugs was thus given to the world in its proper time and into its proper dimension.

We might point out that if you will study the various types of inventions or discoveries as they have been brought into your consciousness and into your world, you will be surprised that a great number of these were more or less very blindly stumbled upon by the individual who was pursuing some vague course of consciousness. He did not know at the time exactly what he was doing; but there was some sort of an intuitive concept within his innermost nature which seemed to prompt or motivate him. He became so engrossed in this procedure as to completely eliminate any outside or exterior values. Thus he was able, in some blind or groping fashion, to stumble eventually upon the principle of truth, or to compound the element which he was striving to bring into the world.

A much more logical course to pursue would be one in which the individual, if he were in the pursuance of such projects, could be properly trained or integrated with the concept of clairvoyance. He would, in the inward consciousness of his own self, contact and construct within the dimension of his own relative being, the factors which were most necessary or vital and pertinent to the advancement of mankind at that time.

It is in this corridor, which is devoted to various types of medical and psychiatric sciences as expressed in the different terrestrial dimensions, that I would like to point out one device which could be of very great value to the scientist of the earth; or rather should I say, a series of devices which are quite electronic in nature. In a future visitation and transmission, you will also see similar devices which are used as inductive instruments in the educational field of relationship of the human being which may be used in other terrestrial dimensions. Here, however, these inductive devices, as we shall call them, are used in the field of corrective medicine and therapy, and use supersonic rays, or frequencies, which can help or heal the individual. These modulated frequencies can be of the philosophical and spiritual nature that can instigate and institute the correct functioning and reasoning processes of the individual and thus induce the corrective therapies into the physical structures of the body.

This type of therapy is used on the planet Mars, not only as corrective therapy, but also in the educational therapies as well. The scientists on your earth today know of the effects of autosuggestion, or the constant repetition of some subject. Although the individual is not conscious of this repetitious autosuggestive transmission, yet he very quickly coordinates this suggestion into the subconscious structures of his being, so that he knows and can repeat whatever is being inductively autosuggestively contrived into his mind at that time.

However, I see that I am beginning to exceed my time limit, which is so important in these transmissions. The subject of this type of instrumentation, which is electronic or vibratory in nature, is in itself, one which is just beyond the horizon of the present concept or doctrine of the physician on the earth today. There is much electronic instrumentation going on at the present time which relates to different therapeutic values, such as those contained in the various spectra of light, as in the infrared or ultraviolet. These, in turn, are superimposed into the human body by such electronic contrivances as light, or X-ray machines, or other types of inductive therapies which are induced by capsules of radioactive material or by such salts or compounds of isotopes of radioactive substances. X-rays or radium rays or various other very highly radioactive substances, such as cobalt, are also used in some instances to destroy cancer tissue.

It would be much better if a corrective therapy could be instilled into the patient's mind, and the proper continuity of the life forces could be so instituted in the human being, that the cancer did not occur. The ounce of prevention here, too, is very valuable; and the person would not have had to incur the predisposition of the cancerous tissue, or the extreme embarrassment and repercussion of the operation, had he been suitably educated in the precepts of the higher dimensions; or had there been practitioners who had relieved the patient in the psychic consciousness of obstructions and blocks which superimposed the cancerous conditions into the patient's body.

The same type of therapy, the same type of reasoning, learning, logic, and wisdom could be carried on into any one of the hundreds of ills and physical disturbances which beset the human body. So the physician of tomorrow will be, indeed, a person who has a great deal more knowledge of the human being than he possesses today. The horizon of his concept will extend beyond fields which are not now conceivable in the dimension of his medical training. However, until such time in the future, let us rest.

— Hippocrates

CHAPTER 84

Greetings to my dear brothers and sisters on the earth. I am another of the old, long-white-bearded men who have been following you around at different times during the recent years (clairvoyantly, I mean). My personal identity, as I was known on the earth, occurred somewhere a few hundred years before the advent of Jesus, I was known at that time as Pythagoras, and as your history books will tell you, I had a great deal of interest in numerology, mathematics, music, and such kindred sciences and philosophies.

It was in the various pursuances of these sciences that I was to be of some use and virtue to mankind in general. My purpose at this time is to lead you into another section of this vast portion of the city of Parhelion, so that you may more suitably be guided through and made acquainted with our order of function and relationship to mankind, as he exists in the numerous planetary systems.

I am purposely trying to proceed rather slowly in the word formations, so that our dear Sister will not be too embarrassed with the process of translation. (Very often the sentences would flow so rapidly that it was most difficult to recapture them from the tape.) My worthy brothers, Hippocrates and Apollonius, are, in themselves, very dynamic and are quite often interjected and infused with an abundance of enthusiasm to such a degree, that they seem to be darting around more or less like fireflies in their dimension. But I shall proceed rather cautiously so that you will not be overburdened with what you are about to witness at this time.

Now, in my section where I, among other teachers teach, we are not overburdened, or shall I say, that we do not have anything spectacular for you such as the very wiggly eel-like formations of thought-form bodies. Our dimension of expression and teaching is related to some of the sciences with which I was closely associated upon the earth, such as music, or numerology, or mathematics, or other laws and orders which you might call physical, or laws of harmonic relationship.

Now we will enter through this big doorway which is on the opposite side of the center of this great lobby. As you see before you, just as it was in the other section, this area, too, is a huge and vast expanse of a dimension which is covered over or vaulted over by a huge curved ceiling of very wonderful radiant energy. Around and about you, you see that the space is divided into somewhat smaller dimensions, wherein are contained the numerous aspects of these various mechanical, musical and mathematical contrivances which are in use in some of these dimensions.

First, we shall go directly to the section dedicated to what properly can be called music. Here you will see practically every known and conceivable type of musical instrument that is, or has been seen, in existence on the earth at this time.

I have anticipated some of the questions which may be asked. You ask why music is exhibited and taught here, and that it is also taught in Muse and in the other fifth section of Shamballa. So I shall repeat, and interject again the principle of frequency relationship. Remember for just a moment, that there are millions of students and teachers in these various

Shamballas constantly coming and going. To avoid a great deal of confusion and inharmony and to further the betterment of the teachings and constructive evaluation of the numerous facets of life, they must of course be related into the structures of spectrums of frequencies and teachings which are most compatible to certain groups or strata of individuals.

To point out this principle more fully, we shall start by taking a small boy who has begun his existence on the earth plane, and goes with his mother to church. He hears an organist and is very much impressed with the wonderful music; so much so that in his future evolutions he goes to Muse. There he is taught along the lines of musical interpretations on the organ. He will, through numerous incarnations into the earth and back into the various centers, finally come under the direct guidance of some great Adept such as Johann Sebastian Bach, who taught in the fifth section. There he will be related to the organ in such a manner that he will be taught the inductive principles of therapeutics in music, which are stimulating to the soul nature of the uppermost integration of man's innermost consciousness with his inner self through the medium of vibration, which is called organ music.

If the boy pursues his evolution on the organ, he will reincarnate here and will be taught another conclusive dimension of expression upon the organ. By this time he will have mastered all of the known dimensions of interpretation on the organ, as it may stimulate any particular fraction of humanity in whatever dimension that such musical vibration can be used properly to stimulate the processes of healing, whether it is psychotherapy or whether it is physiotherapy; for he is now, shall we say, a master of the organ.

However, somewhere along the way he will have come into contact with other facets of spiritual dimensions, so that he will have begun his evolution in other directions, which are consequential to his coming in contact with these other dimensional expressions. We may say that in the constant linking and relinking of these different expressions in his countless incarnations and evolutions into the integration of these expressions, and in learning them and in being taught them, some day in the course of a million years or so, he will have actually and completely gone through the seven centers of Shamballa and all of their associated dimensions of teaching and learning. Thus, he will have become a master, not only of the organ, but also of all other thought and consciousness.

Thus it was with the Avatar Jesus, who appeared on the earth about two thousand years ago. Now Jesus could have stepped up to your organ, if it had existed two thousand years ago, and given a very worthwhile interpretation with his hands upon the keyboard of that great organ. However, with the mastery of all dimensions of consciousness, as expressed from the Shamballas, he would not have needed thus to use the organ, even if it had so existed.

The mere power and dominion of His mind and the relationship of the power and wisdom with which He had so connected and related Himself, gave Him a vast and powerful grasp of celestial interpretation in the field of infinite application of the therapeutic values of God's own Supreme Consciousness. He was therefore able to interject into the consciousness of the individual, through a principle of mind projection, the correct therapeutic values, not only of the elements of the music such as those the boy had learned, but also in consequence all of the therapeutic values of all wisdom of the entire seven Shamballas. And thus the individual could not have been anything but instantaneously healed, with this complete manifestation and deliverance of this infinite wisdom and power.

Now, if you will think for a moment, upon the things which I have just told you, you will begin to see why it is that we seemingly reproduce a great deal of that which has been done previously in some sections. This all resolves itself into a general consensus of evaluation in the concept of teaching and learning, whereby the student gains the proper wisdom and its proper relationships into whatever dimensions he, at the present time, is best able suitably to function, and which will best integrate this knowledge and wisdom in his own structure of the superpsychic body. This also avoids a great deal of confusion which might otherwise occur, had we grouped all of these learnings and teachings under one vast vaulted plane or dimension.

The student might, as a consequence, wander around willy-nilly without the governing factors of frequency relationship. He might quite likely, just as he does upon the earth, wind up in a rather badly confused state of consciousness. The average individual upon the earth is subjected, as I have said, to this willy-nilly type of philosophy. Very often in the first threshold of precept or consciousness in his own dominion, he will start to take onto himself, small portions of other people's interpretations. He thus wanders around in a rather haphazard manner or form; and as he wanders about, he becomes more and more confused, so that he will sooner or later come to the time and the place where he must back out and back away from all this confusion, and come in at some other point.

He will, just as Jesus said, come unto the principal of Infinite Concept "as a little child," or without
any of these presupposed or superimposed concepts
of consciousness within the domain of his own individual structures. In other words, he lays aside these
garments of the false worlds about him, and presents
himself to the Immortal Consciousness as an absorb-
ant sponge, whereby he can immediately begin to absorb into his intellect from the proper place, which is
of the utmost importance. The higher principles of
Infinite conception and perception are not always
suitably inducted into the consciousness of an individual if he is lying in the gutter in a drunken stupor.

Proceeding along this corridor of various types of
instruments, you will see many here which are reminiscent of types of instruments seen before. In fact,
they are facsimilies of the instruments which are in
use upon the earth at your time. You will also see
orchestras which are functioning somewhat as the
symphony orchestras do. This is, in itself, a rather
broad concept of man's own inward struggle to interrelate properly the different harmonic structures of
his own nature within himself.

The music of Bach would not appeal to every individual, but only to a comparatively small group.
However, there must, by necessity, be a great number
of people who know and play the piano and the organ, and different types of musical composition,
which have their own appeal and impact into the
nature of the individuals in the inspirational fashion
for which they are so contrived. In the symphony
orchestra we see an aggregation of musical instruments which are so compounded and integrated
that they play music in such a cohesive or a relative
fashion, that they integrate within themselves, a vast
frequency spectrum of appeal to a great number of

individuals.

We can say that as a whole, the symphony orchestra would appeal to even a greater number of people in its interpretations than would the organ. The symphony orchestra is also much more ductile and elastic in its interpretations of different harmonic chord structures.

Here is an interesting little story which I think you may enjoy, relating to a time in which I took a journey to India during my life upon the earth. It was while I was there, that I found that their interpretations of music, as they were handed down, certainly must have been derived from original concepts which were taught from Shamballa, as it existed on the earth a million years ago.

The average Hindu, as you call him today, had a much higher interpretive value of music and harmonic chord structures at that time, than even exists in your time among the most advanced musical thinkers. The present-day diatonic scale, with its original component of eight notes and their compounding of these various eight notes into the different chord structures and sharps and flats, as they exist in the expressions in different instruments, are in themselves of an infinite variety and number.

The Hindu, however, is not hampered in any sense of the word, by the original inception or confining effects of eight musical notes, as they are in the diatonic scale. In the beginning, he has chord structures of original fundamentals at his command, which involve hundreds of chord structures that are in no way, or in no wise, hampered by any dimensions or concepts. The interpretations or the deliverance of these musical interpretations as vibronics or vibrational chord structures are in themselves most unusual and productive of almost miraculous results.

835

An old trick of Caruso's was to tap on a glass and to reproduce with his voice the original frequency vibration, so that it shattered the glass by superimposing the vibration within the glass. This principle of harmonic induction was well known to the teachers of the various philosophies, as they were conceived in the Buddhistic or Brahmistic concepts, or as they were originally brought down from the Shamballas in the transcripts of the Vedas.

In its true relative way and in its fashion, music was of great service and value in the therapeutic elements of the life of the individual, as he lived in his village or community among the other members of the race or civilization. Any traveler who has gone to India, has seen some fellow sitting on a mat of straw playing upon a flute, with a large woven jar in front of him, and has seen the hooded head of a cobra rising above the neck of the jar weaving back and forth in a rather fascinated fashion.

This is a rather crude way of illustrating to you of what value the inductive principle of music has in vibrating the various molecules or atomic structures within the body; whether it is within that of the snake or that of the human being, it makes no difference. The laws of harmonics and frequency vibration extend to all the different realms of perception and consciousness, whether they are compounded physically, spiritually, or psychically.

In your present world and in your own dominion, sound is just beginning to come into general usage and effect. In the Age of Reformation, sound was expressed in the vast upsurge and upheaval of the very well known and immortal compositions of such composers as the "three B's" as they are sometimes called—Brahms, Beethoven, and Bach—as well as others who were none the less great.

The operatic composers and their hundreds of different interpretations of life in the classics of music were interwoven about the facets of life as it existed at that time. These things are of such inestimable value that they cannot be properly placed in the ordinary concept of the individual, for they played a very vital part and were a real effect in the liberation of man's consciousness in that era and time.

Your own age has not been productive of such musical genius or talent for the simple reason that it has been largely supplanted by a great deal of mechanization. It is in these processes of mechanization and in the exploitation of mankind in the mad race and struggle for survival, that man is gradually beginning to lose the natural instructive relationships with his higher consciousness. He has regulated himself into such a tailored fashion, that he lives, moves, eats, sleeps and breathes within an artifacted air or in a contrived way of civilization, which has superseded anything which has existed upon the earth in your time or in many other periods of history. This, man calls civilization.

There is a notion on the earth in regard to this state which to us presents something of a humorous nature. The picturization of the future man is that his arms and legs and body will dwindle and that his brain will enlarge in such proportions that he will eventually wind up with nothing else but simply a brain.

There are other things which man has thought that he will gradually evolve into, if he continues his course or his pursuance, into the various sciences which he is at present trying to solve, in the conquest of space, or in the submicroscopic regions of atomic structures. I would like to say that this concept is extremely ludicrous, and is not even humorous in its aspect, as man is not in any sense of the word, sufficiently constructive in his thinking to even begin to arrive at some point where his brain will begin to outweigh the necessary balance of virtues which are contained in his physical body. If at any time man does evolve into such an individual which is basically motivated by the more constructive processes of thinking, he will have passed beyond a stage of evolution where he could even be considered an archangel.

We, at no time during the ascension and evolution into the higher spiritual realms, ever decrease for one moment our proper relationship or our aspects as to the relative scale of values which are contained in that which we might call the humanitarian aspects. We can be just a little more compassionate, a little more understanding, and a little more properly constituted in our relationship to our fellow man in the passing and in the reinception of each new evolution into our consciousness.

Simply because we lay aside some of the superstructures and superficialities of the physical world, does not mean that we separate ourselves from the vital motivating factors which are contained in God's own infinite nature. The infinity of that nature creates in itself a relationship of brotherhood between all of His children; and therefore they are truly integrated with each other in thought, word, and deed.

The basic concept of music in producing harmonic chord structures which are inspirational or therapeutic in a more physical relationship within the dimension of man's consciousness upon the earth is, in itself, one of the numerous types of expressions which are very necessary to man in his evolution. In the pure and ultimate dimension and in the abstract consciousness, such conclusions as I have pointed out will ultimately reside within the dominion of the innermost nature of man as logic, reason, and constructive thinking.

Now, let us return to the more scientific relationships of music with man as he exists upon the earth plane at this very day. If you study the science of vibration or harmonics in a strictly electronic field of research, in what is properly called high fidelity in the present day and age, you will find that this inception which has been recently introduced into the thinking of mankind on the earth is, in itself, part of an evolution of science or a metamorphosis of man's thinking into some of the higher dimensions of consciousness. The mere act of thus sowing the seeds of science among men is the more elemental or the beginning stages of his evolution.

As you can picture it in the homes of the average persons who live in America today, even the small boys can talk rather broadly in terms of high fidelity. Everyone knows that high fidelity merely means the ability of certain types of electronic equipment to reproduce properly the frequency spectrum which is within the range of hearing of the human being to a much greater degree, and without the various harmonic frequency distortions which are the natural byproduct of mechanical and electronic reproductive processes.

Generally speaking, the spectrum inception within the human being lies somewhere within the range of from forty to fifteen thousand cycles a second. This, we say, merely means the coming and going of a certain frequency at the rate of so many times per second. A moment's thought will convey to you that it is a very easily conceived principle of sound translation, something like the familiar tossing of a stone into the middle of the pool. We can say that the waves occur and recur at a certain number of times per second.

Likewise, music travels in your dimension in that particular fashion. It actually, shall we say, beats upon the drum of the ear and reproduces, through the mechanism of the inner ear, the necessary impulses of the nerve centers which relate it to the central portions of the brain, and thus sound is produced.

In a broader or much more expanded concept, sound is said to also be partially inductive, not only within the ear, but within the bone and muscle structures of the body. The higher frequencies, for instance, those beyond the realm of twelve to twenty thousand cycles per second, are very often more easily conveyed into the concept of human realization as bone induction, through some of the smaller bones which compose the head. That is why a woman, who is usually more sensitive to those very high vibrations than a man, will very often raise her arms, put her fingers in her ears, and scream when she hears a carpenter filing a saw. Now, even though she has clapped her hands over her ears, she can still feel certain frequencies or sounds which come from these highly pitched noises produced by the file upon the teeth of the saw. She can feel them on her teeth, for they will make her teeth hurt, or they make her feel as though she wishes to grind them together; so that she is actually inductively conveying into her nervous system and into her mind through the various bone structures of her head, some portion of those frequencies which are of the highest pitched nature.

The same principle is understood from the lower spectrums below that which are called the base tones. These are inducted into the various portions of the anatomy, for example, into some of the muscles, and particularly, into the solar plexus or the central region of the abdominal cavity. Some very loud and continued vibrations of the more repercussive instruments around the frequency vibrations of twenty or thirty times per second can, and very often do, make some persons so violently ill that they regurgitate the contents of their stomach.

A moment's thought upon what vibrotherapy can do to the human body, is again reflected in some of the more recently conceived electronic devices which are now beginning to be used in the clinics in some of the American hospitals. These reflect very high frequencies of the order of five or six hundred thousand cycles per second, which are used in the therapeutic treatments of sprains, aches, and such kindred ailments, within the muscles of the human body. The sound itself, in penetrating through this tissue, not only vibrates, but may induce a rise in temperature within the muscular structures, thus creating a great deal more circulation.

The usage of this sound in these high frequency spectrums as a therapeutic agent in the clinics and hospitals of your day is still in a very crude state, and is quite liable to, and sometimes does, subject the patient to severe burns, or may injure him in some other way. If the operator who is using the instrument is not thoroughly familiar with the proper usage of this apparatus, very serious damage could be incurred in the body of the patient.

Light structures, too, have a very therapeutic effect. This is called the science of chromotherapy. If you were momentarily placed within a room which was very brilliantly lighted with an intense violet or purple radiation, you would immediately become dizzy and fall to the floor in a dead faint. The time required for you to become faint and dizzy would depend upon the intensity of the light itself. It merely means that light had so affected you because you could not properly compensate or compromise the proper orientation of frequency within the immediate confines of your own objective consciousness. This produced a distortion of such an intense nature that it completely obstructed the functional orders of integration of mind forces into the body itself; and therefore you became weak and fainted.

Throughout the different Shamballas, starting with Venus, you were continually shown the prismatic, or the lens-like structures which were placed in the ceilings or the roofs of the different classrooms or halls. These lenses or prisms are integrated with the frequency spectrums from the Radiant Infinite Energies about the Cosmic or Celestial Universe. These energies were so projected and infused in their proper proportions and relationships that they actually became food and drink to the individuals who were living and functioning in these dimensions immediately below them.

Man does not need to sustain himself in the earthly process by eating and sleeping to recuperate and revitalize his body in the commonly accepted traditional form of the earth man. If it may bear repeating, there are people living on the earth today who do not need to eat, for they can so regulate their thinking that they become receptive to these Infinite Energies in such a dimensional relationship that they are suitably and properly nourished from the properties within the confines of their own mind.

If you will think for just a moment, you will be able to see that the very coordination or relative factors which motivate the human body, the atomic structures themselves, are sustained from other dimensional sources. By carrying this principle of inductive reception into a higher dimension, you, too, could abstain from the material processes of eating and sleeping to revitalize your body. You could go into a moment of meditation or trance, and suspend or extend your physical consciousness so that its inhibitive factors of relationship to you were thus nullified; so that the Superconsciousness and its superstructures could flow into your body in such a stream of generic energy, that you would be so completely revitalized and rebuilt that you would literally glow in the dark.

The science of chromotherapy and vibrotherapy is relatively little understood in the present day and age in which you are now living. A vast amount of research and learning in the coming years must become necessary to institute properly the orders of energy infusion into your daily lives in their proper therapeutic realm or dimension. However, you have made a start. In the various market places and in the offices of dentistry, medicine, and in other places of reception, there constantly plays a stream of music which is supposedly inductive to the quieter or meditative processes of the individual who is waiting for some type of service, or who is purchasing some articles of merchandise. The music which is being broadcast about the room, or enclosure, is supposed to be selected with the idea in mind that it is conducive, shall I say, to quieting the turbulent emotions within the individual.

You have seen in the pictures of the Greek God Orpheus, that he played the lute in such a manner that it quieted the beasts of the field, so that the lion was able to lie down with the lamb, and other such concepts. It was Orpheus who played his lute when he went into Hades in search of his wife, Euripides; and that he so charmed Pluto that Pluto consented to let him lead his wife back into the domain of mortality upon the earth if he would not look back. Unfortunately, though, he did look back and so his mate was taken from him permanently. We find the same story existing in the St. James Bible; as Lot was leading his wife up the hill from the city of Sodom, she turned back and was turned into a pillar of salt.

However, I am digressing; but I could not help but pause for a moment to interject some of the similarities and pictures of your modern Bible translations into some of the other concepts of the Greek Pantheon. Usually, such legends as they are contained in any concept of mythology or in the translations as they are in the Bible, are merely spiritual, or, shall we say, allegorical concepts. They are, in themselves, strictly parables which relate to certain basic concepts within the innermost nature of man himself.

The picturization of Orpheus was similar to that made possible by my own interpretation of music at the time I lived on the earth in Greece; for when I came back from India, I had somewhat of a knowledge of chord structures. I was able to teach these chord structures to various pupils who lived in the world about me at that time; and these principles of therapeutic values were so contained in these chord structures that they sometimes had very miraculous effects within the immediate confines wherein they were produced.

An angry man, who had murder in his heart, could very quickly be quieted by the striking of some very predominant chords, so that he would be arrested in his mad purpose and could not commit the murder. Miraculous healings also took place by the constant repetition of certain chord structures. The recipient or listener who had some diseased condition, was momentarily transported from certain consequences of vibrationary frequency structures which had diseased the person, so that this chain or chord vibrationary structure was temporarily broken, to the point where the Supreme Energy could remove or heal the condition of the sufferer.

Now here is another very vital and important concept to remember in music, and the composition of chord structures. They are very necessary and relative, inasmuch as the chord structures, in themselves not only reproduce certain harmonic frequencies which are in dimensions particularly pertinent and relevant to the production of certain phenomenal effects in the human body, but also that these various basic fundamental frequencies of chord structures can be modulated with an entirely new or an ultra-dimensional concept of frequency energy. Just as in the principal of your radio, the carrier wave is so modulated that the frequencies of the sound of the voice are properly rectified, simplified and amplified that they can be reproduced upon the cone of the speaker.

So it is, in reproducing certain fundamental frequencies, or sounds, such as in the human voice, that if you are in proper attunement or in the constant relationship with your Higher Self, then the Higher Self, in conjunction with the higher dimensions and the forces which reside within those dimensions, can modulate your voice or superimpose into it, a certain definite number of vibrations, in themselves, tremendously powerful and healing.

The modern man of medicine would quite likely pooh-pooh the idea that you could use your eyes like searchlights for the projection of energy. Yes, this is a very real and scientific fact; it can be demonstrated very scientifically, and without the least fraction of a doubt.

It was so constructed in one of your universities that the students were instructed daily to pass in front of two groups of flower beds. They were told that they must look upon one bed with all the hatred that they could possibly conceive, and curse them inwardly. Then they were to look upon the others with all of the love within their hearts, and bless them fervently. The principal here was strictly propagation of mind energies from the eyes. The students, in passing these two beds of flowers, so inversely or conversely projected the energies of their consciousness into the flowers from their eyes, that the flowers which were blessed grew and became much more profuse in size of the blossoms than those which were cursed or given the doubtful blessings of negation. There are numerous other ways in which the power of projection can heal in the realm of vibrationary frequency transference from a practitioner's eyes, if this person is so in tune and in harmony with his Higher Self.

The hypnotist of this day knows something of these values, and he is very much concerned with gaining the complete fixed attention of the subject, preferably within the domain of his own eyes. However, if you will watch any hypnotist, or if you understand hypnotism yourself, you will be in a state of concentration whereby you will be looking at the patient with a very intent purpose. Whether you know it or not, you will be projecting from your eyes, the twin beams of energy which are coming between the patient's objective consciousness and the subconscious, or the relationary factors in his own conscious nature.

The end result, as you interject your own consciousness through your eyes into the individual's consciousness, merely means that you will temporarily suspend the individual's relationship to himself to such an extent that he will become somewhat of a willing slave, even though he may not know what he is doing in some future time, as he interprets the subconscious inflection of thought that you have implanted into his subconscious mind with the power of suggestion from your voice and from your eyes.

In the future, there will be revelations and translations into the science of chromotherapy and vibrotherapy and such other applications which we call physiotherapy. There are many doctors or practitioners on your earth today, who understand somewhat of the more practical nature and aspect of physiotherapy.

The Romans were devoted to their daily baths, after which the slaves or other members of the household performed the rubbing down process, which is called physiotherapy, whereby the various muscles, tendons and ligaments of the system were so suitably flexed that the person seemed to be a good deal more comfortable, and relaxed. Actually, there is a great deal more to physiotherapy than the mere manipulation of tendons or of bone structures.

If you could see the aura of an individual from a clairvoyant's conception of it, you would see that it stems from the central portion of the brain, or hypothalamus, extending above and coming down to the sides and meeting at the solar plexus in a great heart-shaped radiant energy path, which is the basic fundamental frequency of the auric structure. The original concept of the heart originated from this heart-shaped auric emanation.

These structures which manifest themselves in different ways, have sometimes been called chakras, such as in the hands and feet, and in the tips of the fingers. These energies can be properly related to such frequency spectrums as the magnetic aura, which relates more to animal magnetism; or to such other frequency spectrums which relates a person to

847

the astral worlds or, as we shall say, to the dimensions of frequency which are autosuggestive in nature, or to the higher frequency spectrums which are strictly spiritual in nature.

The manipulation or the passing of the hands over the human body, in itself, does do certain things to the individual, just as the rotation of the armature within the motor relates the various magnetic fields in the path of the magnetic structures contained within the field of these motors, which are conducive to the turning of the armature so that it generates power. So the actual, or shall I say the intelligent relationship of moving the muscles and limbs of the human body, can generate power within the human being so that he will not only become regenerated and rested, but he will feel tremendously lifted and revitalized.

Also, I would like to point out that this is a very valuable adjunct in understanding the relative concepts in the nature of man, as he exists in the terrestrial dimensions; and with the passing of the flesh, so does the passing usefulness of this knowledge likewise go from him into the spiritual dimension. This basic elemental terrestrial knowledge is constantly supplanted by a higher relationship of spiritual knowledge which stems purely from the concepts of mental propagation; and thus man is able to project propensities and wisdom and knowledge into certain frequency directions or paths, whereby they are constructively integrated with whatever concept he is trying to manifest in the process of constructive rebuilding or such other values of healing as he may, at the present moment, be engaged in reproducing.

As we have been talking, we have been moving down along the central corridor, but I have somewhat neglected the function of describing to our readers just what is passing before us here in our exploration. However, up until this point, we have been somewhat confined to the more or less musical interpretations in the field of the vibrationary sciences of chromotherapy and vibrotherapy.

In the future transmissions, which may come from this particular center, we shall thus relate ourselves to some of the orders of harmonic structures which are relative to man's existence on the earth today. We might also point out some of the other structures of vibration which are, in contrast, very inharmonious and destructive in man's nature.

So for the present time, let us return to our respective positions, so that we may rest.

CHAPTER 85

May we resume? We have come to the plane of relationship of Shamballa which is devoted to inquiry, to synthesis and to various educational aspects. We might pause here momentarily to review some of the various facets and some of the dimensions of concepts into which we have somewhat entered.

We have learned that the earth and the inhabitants thereof, are subject to various types and forms of quite negative energies, or that their expressions in a relative sense are negative. The earth itself, if we can picture it thusly, is a planet swimming somewhat in free space, surrounded by a vast magnetic aura, in which there are great tides of discarnate entities, or humans who have lost the form of the physical flesh.

These people, as persons who have formerly lived in the flesh at some other time on the earth, are more or less in a suspended state of relationship. They have not, at this particular time, arrived at any conclusion or any relationship with any particular dimension, except that they have retained somewhat of an attachment to the earth. The memories of earth happenings and earth indulgences in previous incarnations into that planet, have, to a large degree, anchored them into the magnetic structure of the terrestrial planets.

Many people who are daily and hourly passing from the flesh are joining the multitudes of these unseen and invisible legions, which are swirling about in the void of the space about you. Picture for a moment, if you will, a person who is very firmly attached to the desires and to the consequences of his daily life. In becoming detached from his earthly body, he still maintains a strong disposition to keep on living and to rejoin his physical life. Whether these conditions have been incompatible or whether they have been joyous and have produced an abundance of the standards of living, which would be considered comparatively high, is no concern to the discarnate entity. He has nothing else in his mind which would so relate him to any other dimension in the immediate future. His whole concern is to relive the entire pattern of his life, as he has expressed it for so many years on the earth.

If he has been a shopkeeper or some such person, he goes right on opening up his shop in the morning, sitting through the long hours of the day, and endeavoring to sell merchandise to an invisible customer. Or, he may be peddling his wares about the street, or he may be doing any one of the numerous things with which the average individual may have associated himself in his earthly life.

This line of thought and pattern may continue for many years, until some circumstance may arrive or some relative, teacher, or someone in a higher concept of life may arouse him to his true position. Even so, he may be completely resentful of this fact and may try to relive his earthly life. He may become very revengeful or hateful toward the effort to show him that he cannot arrive at some destination or conclusion of what he now realizes is a sort of suspended state.

We can further enlarge this concept to include the various types of mental and physical prostitutes which inhabit the lower earthly orders, the inmates of the prisons and asylums, those who are in the backwash of the large cities, and in the slum areas. They may be bits of human wreckage which have at no time included anything of an intelligent or spiritual concept in the manifestation of their lives. These people swarm in unseen hordes about the magnetic fields of the lower dimensions of expression around the earth.

This in its true aspect of clairvoyance, is indeed a grim and grisly picture, and one which would likely fill the average individual with a great deal of concern as to the dire consequences concerning his own separation from the flesh. But those who are spiritually minded and disposed to be conscious of the higher principles of life, have no need to fear these unseen hordes of human wreckage swarming about your earth, just as they do about other terrestrial planets. The circumstances of frequency relationship, which will harmonize you with the higher structures of life, makes you invulnerable to the encroaching, the possessing or dominating attitudes of any of these unseen hordes of discarnate entities.

We have also examined the numerous pressures which arise from the governmental systems and from the intercourse in the various facets of social life and structures, as they exist upon the planet earth. This, combined with our previous concept of the discarnate entities, will multiply the foreboding aspect of this whole picture. These unseen forces and these unseen pressures, in themselves, all give rise to numerous distortions and numerous consequences of otherwise unexplained and untold happenings in the life of the individual, if he continues a somewhat reactionary course in his daily existence.

The person who is prone to accept any circumstance or happenstance which may come his way may shrug his shoulders and say that it was fate, or that it was God who was punishing him for some other act or consequence, can be called reactionary. The person who is a little more logically minded and can connect circumstances with cause—or as you may say cause and effect—can definitely relate himself to a higher order of sequence, and in the sequence of expression or the higher order, will come into a great deal more harmony in his existence.

The same principle of harmonic frequency relationship must, and always will, relate man to the most direct introspective portion of his innermost nature. He does not at any time arrive at any destination without having devoted some concentration as to the conclusion of the journey, which will enable him to negotiate the distance between his home and the termination of his journey. So in the sequence of his evolution, he must be equally as logical and conclusive in his evolution of life. He should never at any time let the reactionary principles of life replace those which are of the inductive relationships to the higher orders of law, order and harmony as they exist in God's higher dimensions.

Now that we have examined some of the more scientific relationships of sound and vibrotherapy, let us pursue further our analogy and synthesis of life, in your own particular realm and dimension.

Let us continue under the heading of distortions. The unseen worlds of entities about you do produce certain distortions of the individual, and can, in consequence, effect an even more advanced type of thinking in an indirect way, just as the governmental orders of law and social intercourse are correspondingly governed by the majority of the masses of the people as a definite level of mental relationship. However, this need not guide the destiny of any particular individual, who thinks constructively, or at least partially so, in a higher level of intelligence or in continuity. He will very quickly find that there are corrective measures which will not only prevent the recurrence of negation, but will also greatly lessen any shocks which are incurred in the natural consequence of negation which is about him in the terrestrial dimensions.

We say in high fidelity, in the reproduction of music, whether it is from mechanical or electronic sources, that unless we fully hear all the properly balanced portions of the various spectrums of related music and the reproductions of the various instruments, that any omissions of any reproductions will, in the consequence of trying to replace these portions in the relationships of our own minds, induce a sort of mental fatigue. This produces a distortion, just as would the various harmonic frequencies which are regenerated and have no relationship to the original fundamentals.

This also is called a type of intermodulation distortion. These, too, generate a certain peculiar type of irritation or statically charged energy which resides in the individual's magnetic auric structures. Other distortions which arise in your daily life, come from such compounded fractions of energy which are statically charged when you move about and which are generated by the process of your clothing rubbing about upon each other and upon portions of your body.

The friction of the atmosphere, as you pass from one place to another, will also help to create static charges. Even the act of combing your hair generates static charges of electricity. If you shake hands with another person, he may very thoroughly saturate you with a very high charge of negative electricity. Or you may inadvertently bump against someone on the street or in a shop and that person, too, can thoroughly supercharge your entire magnetic structure with a condition which may even make you quite ill.

Now there are certain ways in which these types of static energies can give rise to distortions in the way in which we feel and the way in which we conduct ourselves. The old Yogi understandings and the Vedic concepts, as they stemmed from the original Shamballa and were handed down from generation to generation, were also impounded into the Egyptian and even into the early Grecian philosophies.

There are various methods of discharging these static energies which cause fatigue in the body and mental structures. A higher concept would be to discharge this static condition through a direct principle of reciprocation within the individual consciousness.

More convenient methods which do not require particular moments of meditation or concentration would be to discharge these elements of energy by touching some grounded object, such as a lamp post, or by walking barefoot through the grass, or by ducking into a convenient washroom and running cold water over your hands. All these methods will help to relieve these conditions. It would also be advantageous to the individual if he could keep his fingers crossed over the solar plexus while engaging in conversation with some person who is negatively minded. These things in themselves may seem like silly superstitions; but they are very real and very definitely founded upon concepts of energy transference and relationship.

Now let us consider some more of these unnoticed and unseen distortions which are in this world about you. Too bright sunshine, as you know, will make a person sneeze. The impact of the light into the sensitive regions of the eyes and the nose react sometimes violently to produce such a spasmodic discharge.

Bright sunlight itself has a considerable effect upon the aura of the individual; for each individual is, more or less, definitely related in the types of frequency spectrums to different portions of the light frequencies. The actinic rays, which are the "sun-burning" portions of the spectrum of the sun, are particularly violent to people who are of a psychic nature; and people who have very thin fair skins should be very cautious in their exposure to the actinic rays.

Other persons who have chromatic substructures in the subsurface of the skin, such as the dermatic cells of color as they exist in the colored people, are much more protected in their nature. However, you must know that the colored persons can become sunburned just as can the person who has a much fairer skin. The actinic rays penetrate far deeper than the chromatic layers or cells in the subcutaneous layers of the skin. This, too, is another relationship which could be born in mind to some advantage in the transition of your daily affairs in the manipulations of various life processes.

Machinery, such as the automobile which you drive down the street, while it seems apparently to be a very cleverly contrived and engineered vehicle as a mass of metal, fabric, and rubber, and to be entirely without harm in itself, yet this automobile can, and does sometimes react very violently within the magnetic structures of the average individual. In some instances, the jostling of the body against the seat covers, unless the fabric has been treated or woven for special purposes, may generate such tremendous static discharges in the individual's aura, that he may be shocked by grasping the door handle.

There are also other factors which create tension

when you are riding in your automobile. The various vibrating and reciprocating mechanisms, as the wheels are journeying over the pavement, in itself generates a tremendous amount of high frequency and static electricity of a nature which is almost too high a potential to be properly recognized. This in itself has a somewhat tiring and depleting effect upon the individual.

The mere concentration of driving the automobile down the highway is not, after a days journey, the sole contributing factor in creating fatigue in the individual. Instead, as I have said, it is the regeneration of these high frequencies which have tended to fatigue the driver by partially interfering with his normal process of regeneration and recuperation.

Briefly, and in short, if you look about you in your daily life, you need to make certain compromises. If you need to bend your will, or to adjust in some way to any differences, you can rest assured that there is some very definite repercussion in your psychic makeup, for you will need to continue to readjust yourself to compensate yourself for that particular facet.

We might say to the housewife who is using her vacuum cleaner, that she is very often unconsciously subjected to intensely high frequency radiations, which are of an unseen and even unnoticed dimension of frequency relationship. Even the scientist who produced and developed the motor within the vacuum cleaner was not aware of the sequence of the multiples of regeneration in the higher harmonic frequency structures.

The old ancient, who walked in a pair of sandals, or in bare feet, upon the hillside and ate fruits and vegetables as they came natively from the soil, and who dressed more or less in clothing which was hand woven from the fibers crudely grown and harvested from the wool of sheep, was in a much better position to live quietly and harmoniously than the man who has so surrounded himself with the numerous appurtenances of this civilized world. This more primitive style, while it may not be entirely suitable or compatible to your way of evaluation, yet, in itself, it was not one which would by necessity incur these various indispositions or distortions in your nature, or subject you to various reincarnations and to the possibility that you might become, shall I say, hung upon one of these astral planes, where you would seem to be without the power of progressing either forward or backward, although you would actually be going backward.

If you have ever had a nightmare where you seemed to be wanting to get away from something but lacked the power of motivation, then that is the way some of these discarnate entities would feel in their present state of relativity.

Now looking about your great cities on the earth (and I am not excluding any nations), and in the functioning of these cities, with the various and numerous multiplicities of all the mechanical contrivances of both an electronic and purely mechanical nature, there is generated and regenerated these higher orders of harmonic frequencies, and as they are generated and regenerated into such frequency spectra without the dominant and controlling relationship which regulates them into such a dimensional form of transition, they are not made intelligible or useful in any way. These energies therefore can be said to be free-willed, and as they are potential energies, they must travel; and, coming in contact with other energies or other frequency spectra which are intelligent in nature, they are liable to produce very violent clashes and produce regenerations of other harmonic frequencies which can be equally destructive or incompatible to any life which may exist in the immediate vicinity.

Even the mere act of oxidation upon a surface such as iron, or the paint upon your buildings, is not always determined as a direct chemical fluctuation of certain atomic structures within the elements of oxygen or iron, as they are so constituted. The basic degenerative effects of such oxidation are contained partially within outside influences which are radiated from these high frequency dimensional structures. Iron will rust much more freely and much more completely in a city than the same piece of iron would rust in the outlying suburban areas.

There are other things which effect the life of the city dweller, as he is in constant contact with tremendous precipitations of chemical substances which flow freely in the air. At the present time the precipitations which you call smog, in the atmosphere of the numerous cities, have created a health problem which is one of national importance and one which is trying the minds, the wills, and the patience of all citizens and executives in the functioning of these cities. We cannot over-emphasize the deleterious effect of this chemical smog on the physical constitution of the human being, which is also aided and abetted by the supersonic frequencies of the other types of smog which I have just mentioned, and which are byproducts of the manipulative mechanisms.

In addition, the degenerative thought sequences of the individuals are also a very vital and contributing factor to this general smog problem, as it exists in the cities. The unseen and the unsmelled, or the undetected fog which is in the spiritual dimensions or the astral dimensions, is much more potent and much more dangerous than the type which you see and smell about you, which is generated largely by byproducts of petroleum combustion.

Even if your cities were entirely free and clean from the effects of the smog generated by the internal combustion of motors and other products of petroleum refineries and other various types of combustible materials, still your cities would be plagued by the generation of the numerous frequencies, which are beyond the range of detection. Such are the problems of your electronic and mechanical contrivances.

The thought processes in the field of negative thinking are, in themselves, a subject which requires a vast concentration of analysis and thinking for proper evaluation. This is the type of smog with which a person comes in contact in a more psychic way. The combustible byproduct smog is one which is breathed into the lungs and absorbed into the skin; whereas the other type of smog is, in a way, absorbed in a more psychic relationship through the acts and consequences of conducting your daily lives. If you could properly maintain a completely introspective attitude toward these outside influences you might remain somewhat aloof from these dense seas of smog which are surrounding not only your cities, but in some sense of the word, the entire globe.

It is fortunate indeed, that God in his Infinite Wisdom has so regulated the processes of the functioning of various dimensions into such frequency spectra that from one frequency spectrum to another, there is a complete line, or a separation; and in the multiplicities of these frequency spectra, there is, in a sense of the word, a complete freedom and isolation from the effects of any other frequency spectrum. However, this is largely dependent, as I previously explained, upon the factors of harmonic relationship, or upon a regeneration or degeneration of such frequency spectra which very often link each other in such a fashion, through the law and order of harmonic relationship.

I feel by now that you are all more or less mentally throwing up your hands and saying, "My goodness! I wonder if there is any chance at all for me to survive the many deleterious aspects in my world and my dimensions. Is there any hope that I may, as a consequence, resume a continuity in my evolution and arrive at some state of spiritual integration with my higher self?" Yes indeed, there is a great deal of chance. In fact, there is more of a chance that you should arrive at some such frequency destination than that you should remain, shall I say, at the bottom of the pile and continually be regenerated into a world of cause and effect.

The moment that you begin to evaluate your life constructively into such a fashion or sequence, or into such a way whereby you can see a sequence into higher dimensions, and whereby you can so link your mental faculties with the higher dimensional orders of relationship, then you will have begun at that same moment to free yourself from the obsessive relationships of the terrestrial dimensions, and you are thus on your way upward.

However, at no time and in no position must you pause and rest on your laurels, because you have achieved some form of relationship with a higher order or dimension whereby you feel temporarily peaceful or complacent in your mind. Do not think for one moment that this is the end of the battle. The victory is won only at the price of eternal vigilance; and for that you must work constantly and constructively and positively in the direction into which you must surely evolve in your spiritual consciousness. There are no short cuts in this way other than the short cuts which you could visualize within your own mind; and you should arrive at a position whereby you could constructively utilize the great powers of mind force which lie untapped within the dimensions of your Superconscious Mind. Until that period in your evolution of life where you can fully realize the full power of your Superconscious Self in its true dimensional relationship, then only can you envision that you, too, could do just as did Jesus—walk through seemingly solid substances of the earth, and upon water, or through fire, or through any of the kindred substances which may lay waste to the average individual.

So, dear friends, we have presented some of the aspects and relationships of your terrestrial dimensions to you purely upon the premise that by acquainting you with these various factors, you could become intelligent in your reactions against them; or that you could become intelligent in forming some defense by creating a positive and constructive purpose in life; and that this defense against all of these various dimensions of negative energy in your own world, lies in the pure act of positive consciousness in the daily transitions of your life.

If you can do everything positively, think everything positively, and know it is concluded in the highest premise of intellectual functioning, and that everything is regulated in God's Infinite Mind and related into different perspectives according to the law of order, harmony, and frequency, then you are insulating yourselves thoroughly and completely against the obsessive and corrosive actions of the negative planes of relationships. This is the only way in which it can be done. There is no one who can do this for you, because you are there on the terrestrial plane for that one and only purpose.

You shall never leave those terrestrial dimensions until you do so by the power of your own will, and by the constructive evaluation of your own thought processes. There is no place in God's great Universe where a person can float about on a pink cloud and play a harp and be entirely unrelative to that dimension. Each person must learn to live, to act, and to relate himself with God's Infinite Mind and to achieve the Infinite relationship and the knowledge contained in that Mind before he can live in the proximity in which these things are, in their own way, relatively perfect in their expression.

As it has been pointed out, the average savage who lives in his wattled hut in the jungle and worships before the door of the witch doctor, would feel very ill at ease living in one of your modern bungalows. He would not know what to do in the various orders and functions which are contained in such a house. The bathroom, for instance, would be a place of holy terror to him. He would not know how to conduct himself were he to go through a church door. The whirring sound of your mixmaster or your washing machine or your vacuum sweeper would quite likely send him into a frenzy, if he had not become acquainted with these things, or if he had not, in some way, conceived them in his mind. If you have studied the exploration and the ways of some of the older explorers, you have learned that a simple mirror in his hands would often send a whole tribe of savages fleeing into the woods; or the striking of a match would make him a veritable god upon the throne of worship in their village.

You also, in a dimension which God, in His Infinite Wisdom and Intelligence, had so created, would find that it would be as unrelative to you as your world is to the savage. You could function there no more intelligently than could the savage in your cities. You must arrive at the conclusion of this evolution for the purpose of learning and coming into contact with God's Infinite Mind before you can reside in close proximity with Him.

Until a further discussion, my friends, we shall rest with the pure essence of God's Love.

— Pythagoras

CHAPTER 86

My dear ones, I shall first bow to the usual custom of identifying myself as the individual who once lived upon the planet earth and received the spiritual messages of truth underneath a fig tree. I lived about five hundred years before the advent of Jesus. Personal identity in these higher dimensions, however, does not mean the same relationship with the Infinite Mind Intelligence of God. However, this has been somewhat pointed out to you in previous discussions and I shall consider time as wasted in further explanation.

We shall head this particular transmission under the title of "Personal or Humanitarian Relationship." It has been so contrived within the fabrication of this book, and in the numerous previous transmissions, that we shall not only acquaint man with the higher natures and dimensions of the vast terrestrial and celestial universes about him, but that we can also acquaint him with the proper paths of progress.

As it has been determined in the factors of evolution into which the planet earth is now revolving, the Eastern and Western worlds are at the present time, very strongly divided. Between these divisions there exists also another level or a dimension of intelligence which is strongly opposed to either the expression of the Eastern minds or the Eastern peoples and those of the Western world.

Within these divisions can well exist a potential

destructiveness, which could obliterate man from the earth. We, therefore, are making a very serious attempt at some sort of reconciliation in joining together the forces of men's minds into a universal concept or pattern of spiritual relationship. We believe that man can ultimately work out his destination and achieve what has been called Nirvana, or the junction of the individual consciousness with the Supreme Intelligence of God.

We shall start somewhere with the migration of the Aryan race from the original plains of Mongolia into the plains of India, and in the mingling of the peoples who were already living there, there occurred great conflicts of an emotional nature which developed into a very complex caste system. Arising from out of the dust and debris of human emotionalism at that time, the Brahmanic concepts were formed, wherein the Brahmans were the caste masters, and beneath them were the subservient castes, which were integrated and interwoven into an extremely complex and non-sensical existence of life.

Previous to the time of my birth, there had been born in India an individual by the name of Mahavarah. He himself was a Brahmist caste lord and extremely cruel and vindictive in nature. It was from the guilt complexes of his inner mind, that he became somewhat of a spiritualist as well as the militant leader of the people and became known as Jain, the Conqueror. It was Jain who taught the people, from the extreme junctions of his own guilt complex, that it was wrong to eat flesh, and to kill even so much as a small fly, even though he himself had been guilty of many crimes.

And so it came to pass that the concept of Jainism was born. People further extruded this consciousness into such concepts as they believed a junction with heaven or some other place could be very quickly obtained by the infliction of a great deal of mortal suffering within their bodies. And so, for the purpose of self-punishment and self-infliction to gain the higher states of consciousness, many individuals went about with skewers thrust through their cheeks or with needles and hooks hanging about their bodies in great numbers. They would lie for many hours in the hot sun on a bed of sharp spikes or do numerous other things which they believed would help them or to rectify the condition of atonement within their minds.

In studying the history of Buddhism and the biography of my life at that time, you will see that I was born of a Brahmanic merchant, and was possessed of considerable wealth and family. It was during my excursions about in the province in which I lived that I was shocked by finding these very perverted expressions of so-called religious beliefs. So, I set about in my own way to try to bring some sort of rectification or enlightenment into the minds and hearts of the people.

At first I tried the beggars bowl, but could never reconcile my mind to the idea of God manifesting himself into such an abject state of consciousness, and that this in itself was foreign to the complete concept of ultimate realization. It was in this state of meditation and under my very familiar fig tree in the square, that I suddenly perceived that the true dominion of consciousness came from within the individual, and that in the numerous evolutions, or shall I say karmic or pranic structures of life, that man would and could arrive at the junction of consciousness with the Supreme Creator, which was called Nirvana.

Now fired with a new purpose and a new concept, I went about the land to try to untangle the minds of the people and instill a very simple concept of self-realization. In the beginning it was remarkably like the concepts of metaphysics and the simpler truths which are in existence today. As it later developed into Buddhism, and, if you will study the structure of Buddhism as it was taught and so derived from these concepts in the years following my leaving the earth, you will find that it did follow in many ways, parallels of the teachings of Jesus or the teachings of Moses.

There was the Eight-Fold Noble Enlightened Path, which in itself was a compound structure of thirty-seven divisions of Arahatship, wherein the individual could find for himself certain dominant principles of spiritual structures, whereby he could conceive and regulate his life into some such higher dimension. Within this Arahatship was combined the elements of truth and error, which are still used in several of the Mind Sciences of your day and time.

Man was taught the dissociation of life and the concept of mentality of the individual away from such destructive paths which were materialistic in nature; also, that he should continually, within his mind, strive for the dominion of consciousness which would further his evolution into higher dimensions of consciousness.

There is in the transcripts of some of the disciples who followed after me, the context of Three Baskets of Bread, or the Pitakas. In these Three Baskets of Bread is found something very similar to that of the Synoptic Gospels of the dispensation of the New Testament. There is also contained therein the Ten Commandments, which bear a remarkable resemblance to the Ten Commandments of Moses. I am not pointing these things out to you with any sense of personal pride in achievement, but merely on the basis of evaluation that in your own life, you too, in moments of meditation, can and will achieve within yourself, the higher motivating principles of life; and that these principles, within themselves, are of the utmost importance in the life of every individual.

However, in the centuries which followed my leaving the earth, there began in the usual manner, people who would in their own way, interpret and re-teach the simple elements of truth which I had tried to teach them. Therefore this began to give way, to a large degree, to the pantheism of the numerous gods and expressions of the gods, just as they have previously existed in the dominion of the Brahmanic text, previous to my reincarnation into the earth.

It was for this purpose that Shankara was reincarnated onto the earth to try to substantiate the simpler context of truth in the original precepts and dominions of that which is called Buddhism. A further study will reveal that Buddhism in China and Buddhism in Japan have also suffered somewhat in the evolution of time, and that they are distinct offshoots from the original concepts, and that they, too, have suffered much in the numerous and intricate methods of expression.

Here we would like to emphasize and reemphasize the simplicity of the doctrine of self-realization, as it was taught by Jesus and by the numerous Avatars who have lived on the earth in previous times. The simplicity of self-realization transcends any bounds of material expressions which are taught in any temples or synagogues or churches. The individual is not necessarily restricted by such concepts of realization as might be attained in these temples or churches.

The idea of spiritual fellowship, as it could exist, not only among the communities of individuals, but in the communities of nations, must be thoroughly realized before true peace can be achieved on the earth. The unification and sharing of all general principles of spiritual concept must be fully entered into. Every individual, every community, every nation, must realize that they are actually brothers and sisters and, as such, are all equally entitled to the same dominion of consciousness within God's Celestial and Infinite Mind.

There has been in the past, a condition of separation or isolation between the Western minds and the Eastern or Hindu philosophies. There are many obvious reasons why these conditions exist, inasmuch as the Hinduism or Buddhism, as it exists today, is extremely complex in nature. While it does contain the elements of the original Buddhist transcripts, yet it has been enlarged, or shall I say, interwoven with the pantheism of numerous gods; and in the interpretation, has suffered considerable dereliction from the original concept of simplification of man's evolution.

The Western mind could not orientate or adapt such an intricate philosophy of life into the structures of his material world. The American citizen or such citizenry as exists in similar nations, is too thoroughly steeped and indoctrinated in the production of the material values and ways of life. They must see the profits of the day on their ledgers. They have no time to spend in the temples or in the corners of their chambers sitting in postures of meditation, wherein they can separate themselves from the carnal lusts and enter into the Infinite concepts of their inner nature. Nor are these things, in themselves, completely adaptable to any man's way of life upon the earth. The earth, as it exists in its pure capacity of dimensional relationship, is one in which mankind lives on a certain level of intelligence and performs certain functions according to the concept of reincarnation.

Further, to simplify and to strip any idea of complication in the structures of Hinduism as they exist to the scientist and to the Truth seeker, we shall present to you a very simple concept. Much of this has been contained and written into the numerous lines of the preceding pages; but we believe that by repeating truth and by presenting it in different facets of realization, the average individual will come into a fuller realization; or that those who have not yet realized can now conceive the truth.

The structures of spiritual philosophy which are somewhat understood in the Yoga and in other more highly evolved spiritual concepts in India, resolve somewhat into three dimensions. We are concerned with the first or the lowest dimension, which is called the terrestrial or material dimension. A word which is used frequently in India for this dimension is called maya. Within maya, is found all of the elements which constitute the material world, as they are known to the scientist by their respective weights. At our time in India, we called them anas. The scientist of today calls them atoms.

To further understand the nature of material mass or atomic structures, a few more words on this subject would not go amiss, although it has been very thoroughly presented to you. As it has been pictured, the atom is actually a very complex mass of wave forms; and the complexity of this mass depends upon the atomic weight of the individual element. The theory was presented to you that in the evolutionary or revolving vortexes of energy, were produced the hard core nucleus structures of the atom. The earth scientist knows that every element possesses what he calls an isotope. Isotopes, in themselves, are the exact counterpart of the pure or terrestrial atom, with the exception that they do not possess the same quotient of atomic weight. In other words, the density, as it was explained by Archimedes, is a simple law of displacement; and the scientist now knows that the atom can appear or reappear in different atomic weights. This fact has been very puzzling to him, and he has classified these new elements with their different weights as isotopes.

This is very simply explained inasmuch as your concept of the revolving vortexes will now immediately present to you the idea that within the vortexes are contained innumerable dimensions of energy expression or intelligence, which stem from the great central vortex or the Fountainhead, as it is sometimes called in the causal world. Within these numerous manifestations of different dimensional equations of the atom are found the reproductions of the lower or baser nuclei, called the original atomic structure. This is just a little more complex, or a principle which is continued into a somewhat more expanded concept; but it will present to the scientist a proper way to evaluate the atom and so further speed his progress, whereby he can link himself with the proper relationship of the higher order of dimensional transition.

In the second world of the Yoga or the Buddhistic concepts as they are thoroughly understood, we must further dissociate Yoga with Buddhism to this extent: the world of Yoga, in itself, is an extremely advanced state of two combinations of understanding, or, shall I say, two dimensions of understanding. It is the relationship of the higher orders of the causal world in manifesting themselves into spiritual concepts which have given the Yogi the seemingly supernatural powers which were demonstrated by the Avatar Jesus.

I was not, at my time on earth, a Yogi and did not at any time appear and disappear, but lived simply and easily, just as did every one who was on the material plane of consciousness. However, in reappearing into a material dimension as Shankara, I was able to demonstrate somewhat the Yoga principle of the higher attainment of self, such as walking upon water and doing the numerous other things which are considered supernatural, but which are actually only the natural principles of life; for here, too, was demonstrated the conjunction of the Yoga with the Supreme Consciousness.

The second world, or the second dimension, which we shall consider now, is actually being presented to you somewhat as the various octaves or the chords upon some huge keyboard. This second section is the dimension of thought or prana. It is the dimension of intermediate relationship with the higher or celestial dimension, or the causal dimension, as it has been called.

Within the dimension of prana exists energy transition in many other different dimensions and forms, just as in the terrestrial dimension, or the dimension of maya; and you will also see innumerable octaves or chord structures of the transference or transmission of energy as it exists about you in your terrestrial dimensions. When you leave the flesh and go into the world of prana—or as it is called, the astral world, you will see here, too, that although energy does not associate itself as mass, it reappears in a somewhat more intelligent form.

In the world of prana, anything which you may conceive within your mind, can actually and does instantly exist, if you are so properly constituted in your thought processes and that you have conceived within the dimension of your mind that the existence of astral worlds are related to harmonic frequency structures, as they have been explained to you; and that you will automatically regulate yourself into such a dimension or relation of integration within this astral dimension.

Roughly speaking, we can divide the peoples in the astral dimensions into two classifications: those who are first Initiates or those who have reached the place which is called the fork in the road, where they have conceived themselves as something of Infinite conception and purpose; and are thus regulating themselves with the dominion of their minds into different orders of harmonic relationship within the pranic or astral worlds.

Then there are those countless individuals whom we shall call migrants. These are individuals in the lower elemental forms of evolution who have not yet achieved within the concepts of their minds, anything beyond the relative dimension of the material world; and so they continually revolve within the orders of certain regulated frequency spectrums back and forth, much the same as the commuter who leaves his home for his office, and returns at night. The interval of time spent here, however, is somewhat different. Man may start this regular commuting back and forth in periods of 600, 900, or even 1800 year intervals or successions.

When man has somewhat enlarged his concept so that his spirit is quickened, shall I say, he will increase the oscillations or the migrations back and forth into a much faster rate. He will begin reappearing in 300 or even in 150 year intervals. In the time between, when he is in the spiritual dimension, he will revolve in somewhat of a dreamy or catalytic state of transition. He will be living and reliving the countless and numerous terrestrial and physical experiences in a sort of dream world, one of unreality; and as he floats about, he is not quite capable of conveying or conceiving order and harmony and regulation into his concept of mind.

This state is quite different among the first Initiates, who were previously described, since they have conceived somewhat the order and harmony and law in man's dimension. Because they have so regulated themselves into their proper dimensional relationships, they will find life much more highly organized, and to such an extent that they are able to, and frequently do, carry on their lives in a higher capacity than that at which they arrived in their earthly dimension.

As it has been pointed out, these people have not yet evolved into the higher dimensions of the causal world; so they might frequently live and relive, in the astral worlds, their numerous trades and crafts in a higher expression. There they would learn newer and more basic concepts. As they were all more or less in a higher degree of contact or relationship with the higher spiritual or celestial dimensions of causal relationship with the Infinite Mind, therefore their opportunities for enlarging their concepts would consequently be increased in a direct proportion and ratio. This will point out to you some of the more fundamental truths and concepts in that which is called reincarnation or evolution.

Now if we can picture an individual who has evolved through the migrant's state of evolution and has become a first Initiate, he will then consequently evolve or reincarnate numerous times just as he so sees fit. There he rises from the dominion of his will, rather than from a struggle for a certain level of expression. He will see in his evolution, a certain definite purpose or intent and with this reincarnation and plan of pattern he will be able to work out the various negative vortexes which he has conceived within his concept.

It has been explained to you that in the Theosophical beliefs of the earth, man has many different bodies, like the skin of an onion. This is true to a certain degree, if we remember that the skins of the onion are actually certain harmonic frequency structures, or vortexes within the psychic body of the individual and that his own relationship and the life in the dimension in which he lives at the present moment, depends upon the structures of the harmonic frequencies which he may call a body.

After revolving into higher spiritual dimensions, these frequency structures quite naturally cannot, and do not exist in these higher dimensions. And so they are dissipated or rectified, and the individual therefore is rebuilding for himself a psychic body of a higher order of frequency structures.

There are no real lines of demarcation or boundaries between these worlds, rather, they are somewhat like the chord structures in the keyboard of an organ or a piano. They must all relate themselves in certain orders of dimensional equation in the frequency relationship. It is in this way that God can, and does, shine the Intelligence of His Supreme Countenance down into the numerous and infinite number of dimensions which he so conceived in His Mind.

The third dimension of concept is called the celestial, or spiritual, or sometimes the causal expression. It is here that again the same nature of evolution is contained to a much higher order and content, and to a much higher degree, within the individual. Here again certain orders of frequency relationship are entered into whereby the individual is now in a position to have such a concept, that he can visualize instantaneously a great number of things at the same time. He can also enter into processes whereby he can direct the Infinite Energies of God's Great Radiant Mind into whatever constructive orders or artifices which he has so conceived within his mind. He can, if he so wills, construct himself almost immediately a body which will enable him to live upon the earth and that he can reabsorb into the cosmic mind of himself, the constituents of energy which are so contained in that earthly body.

In arriving at this infinite conception, we must bear in mind that this is not a complete infinite conception, for as it has been stated, only God can conceive all things instantaneously; and as God has so conceived all things instantaneously, so He is constructing, reconstructing, realizing, and manifesting all things instantaneously.

In achieving a close relationship of the individual self with the Infinite concept of God, the individual therefore becomes a participating element of God's Infinite Nature, and he takes upon himself the characteristics of this Infinite God, so that there is actually nothing which you might conceive in your finite dimension which this individual could not, or does not do. Nor is there anything which he cannot conceive. However, the ultimate conception always is, and always will be, within the dominion of God's own Infinite Mind. We shall not go beyond this point with you at this time, as this would be a concept which could not be brought within the confines of your dimension at your time.

A further description of the world of prana or the astral worlds would be somewhat in order for the people of the earth, as this means something of the next step of integration in their evolution. These astral worlds, as we have pictured these Shamballas to you, are actually beautiful globes of energy which exist in varying sizes and in numerous frequency structures, all within the definite spectrums, or octaves of chord structures, in their own relationships in the astral worlds. Upon these numerous globes or spheres of astral energies, you will find people of all nations, all races, all creeds, and all colors, living in direct proportions to such concepts and principles of life which they have conceived in their terrestrial dimensions.

It was pointed out to you that man, starting as he does as an Infinite concept from the dimension of God's Infinite Mind, must start in the lowest of the elemental structures of evolution, such as are contained in the terrestrial planet of the earth. In the consequence of his migration or evolution into the higher planes of consciousness, he does contact and re-contact an innumerable and an infinite number of dimensions. In these relationships he finds his true individuality, which will later become the infinite bounds of the dimension of his celestial kingdom or the causal world.

We earnestly wish that it would be proper at this time to present to the earth people, and especially to the Western minds of your civilization of America and other countries, something similar to that which is called the Cinerama in your movie theaters. If we could picture for you on the screen of such a theater, some small fraction, or a peek, into this world of prana, or the astral world, you would be very much impressed. You would see these beautiful spheres of light radiating in their different colors and vibrating and pulsating with the great cosmic energies, and that living upon these various planets are numerous civilizations and hundreds of millions, yes, even billions of people, who have at different times lived in the terrestrial dimensions similar to the earth. You might also picture in these astral dimensions, that something of the nature of time and space had been eliminated from the consciousness of the individual.

Man can, and frequently does whenever he so wishes, evolve into such a higher state of astral or pranic consciousness and is thus enabled to go very quickly from one world to another, even though the dimensions may be, in terms of your earth time, separated by hundreds of millions of light years. Since time and space completely disappear in these higher concepts and orders of frequency relationship, when a person conceives that he is in a place, he is there. If he is a higher Causal or Celestial Being, he can actually be in a number of places at the same time, simply by conceiving within his mind the instantaneous realization of these things.

Now you are beginning to understand why we call the material world, such as your planet, the world of maya, or illusion. It is strictly so because the factors which you call mass and energy, are, in themselves and in their expressions, very confusing to your nature. You have continually tried to orient such concepts in your mind which will relate you to the expression of energy in whatever dimension that it can thus express itself, either as mass or energy.

The equations of these transitions of energy must by necessity resolve themselves into the higher dimensional concepts. They never can and never will be properly evaluated from the terrestrial dimension of man's consciousness. It has been the common mistake throughout the ages of man's history to try to relegate God's Infinite Wisdom into the concepts of his own small world.

The astronomer of your day is just as guilty of this as was the ancient savage in his relationship with the spirit of the earth, fire, and water. The astronomer who postulates the theory that life cannot, and does not exist in other planets and in other dimensions because he cannot conceive other dimensional relationships of energy, is guilty of the same malpractice of thought concept as is the savage in the jungles.

Such concepts are quite vicious in their nature inasmuch as the peoples of the world at your time have set these astronomers and physicists upon some sort of pedestal and have instituted in them certain virtues which they do not actually deserve. It is quite true, however, that the scientists in the material dimension are pushing aside many of these barriers which have impeded man's progress. It is also quite true that they have contributed much to longevity and to many other things which have been called conveniences, or to such contrivances which are supposedly able to lift the burden of toil and strife from mankind. However, they have sometimes been somewhat of a boomerang in nature. To support these false materialistic structures, man has become a slave to this great robot which he has constructed. He would quickly find, and he often does, in the evaluations of consciousness within himself that these things which he has so contrived and must now live with, actually require all of his time and all of his energies continually to support and to reinstate his daily way of life.

Our position upon this tenet of conception is very firm. We do not believe that man in his civilized consciousness as he calls it in his day and time, should as a consequence, immediately lay aside all of these appurtenances of his civilized world even though he could do so. The evolution of consciousness within the individual must always be regulated according to his ability to conceive and to reinstate certain orders of concept within his own mind. If these laws are not thoroughly observed, he suffers a great deal of shock or psychic impact, which is in itself a form of karma; and thus he must, in some future evolution, adjust himself and rectify this psychic impact which is within his nature.

We can only recommend to the individual that his purpose in life shall be one of a more thoroughly ordered and regulated relationship, which will enable him to perceive the ultimate destiny of his spiritual nature in conjunction with the Infinite Mind of God. If he so contrives within his mind to fabricate a philosophy which will thus integrate him with some sort of factual and a continual realization of this element or personal realization with his mind, he will by direct consequence, be a first Initiate. He will very quickly become one of those beings who can migrate into the astral or pranic worlds, and there live upon some such astral planet as will be much more suitable and conducive to him in his mental evolution, further to conceive and induct into his mentality, the higher concepts of God's nature.

I, but using the word "I" rather loosely, shall conclude, not in the evaluations of my own personal interpretations, but shall say to you all in your future expressions of life, either in the terrestrial world or in the world of prana, that the evolution of the world is thus concerned with further propagating man into a higher dimension of relationship and concept which is sometimes called the Aquarian Age. As you will see in your future explorations into the astral planet of Orion, and into Helianthus, that these earthly evolutions are divided into thirty-three regularly ordered cycles, as they are controlled by thirty-three higher dimensions of Causal or Celestial interpretations, which are called Logi.

These thirty-three higher orders of concept or dimensions in the higher Celestial realms are in themselves, shall I say, shedding a certain dominant ray of energy which contains the necessary elements of spiritual integration and leadership into the minds of such individuals who may, at different periods of time, reincarnate into the earth. These cycles are about one thousand years in length, and the evolution of thirty-three thousand years is, in itself, the original concept of that which has been called astrophysics. It means that the thirty-three Logi have so constructed these magnetic lines or rays of light or power or radiant frequency energy into the terrestrial dimensions, that the earth, in its evolution about the sun, intersects and bisects these different radiant energy lines according to the cycle of the recessional. Thus, at thirty-three thousand year intervals, the earth has completely intersected or bisected these thirty-three dimensional rays of light from the thirty-three dimensions of Logi. Although the absolute and direct proportions of these rays or magnetic lines, in themselves, are not felt in a terrestrial dimension, they are the guiding and dominant factors in the mental and spiritual evolutions as they are manifested in the dimensions of mankind as he exists in the earth at that cycle of interpretation.

Just as you saw in the period of the Hellenic Age, so you can trace the courses of history in the pages of your books; and you will see that these various seemingly intersected tides of time actually resolve themselves into somewhat of a more definite and well-ordered relationship. This, too, shall give you a better concept as to how God regulates the vast Celestial and Cosmic dimensions, which are the product of His Mind.

You must also always conceive within yourself that there is nothing happenstance within this Infinite concept; that everything does and has existed from beyond what you call the beginning of time, and will exist beyond what you call the ending of time, for there is neither beginning nor ending. This order, regulation, and harmony, exists throughout all of God's Infinite concepts. It is only in the struggle of evolution of man within himself between the carnal, or the world of maya with the innermost reaches of his spiritual nature, that he has come into the conclusion of confusion. This struggle started for man when he was a primeval savage, and in seeing in the spirits of the earth, air, fire, and water, some relationship to his own spiritual nature, that this struggle within himself was, in his future evolutions, manifested in these terrestrial dimensions in the infinite number of concepts, as they exist in the different interpretations of either political or spiritual orders, numerous creeds, cults, churches and races, which are, in themselves, the result of the strife of man within himself to orient himself into the higher concept and into the higher relationship of his true innermost nature.

This is the struggle for Nirvana. It is the ultimate attainment of each individual to thus become a personal integrated and fractional working part of this Infinite Mind of God.

Until such future time as myself and others here in Parhelion may serve you, I am your humble servant,

— Guatama Buddha

Other works by Ernest L. Norman:

The Voice of Venus
The Voice of Eros
The Voice of Hermes
The Voice of Muse

The Infinite Concept of Cosmic Creation
Cosmic Continuum
Infinite Perspectus
Infinite Contact
Truth About Mars
The Elysium (Parables)
The Anthenium   "
Magnetic Tape Lectures
Tempus Procedium
Tempus Invictus
Tempus Interludium Vols. I & II

Also a publication, now reprinted by
Unarius Publishing Company:
The True Life of Jesus of Nazareth (1899)

(The Sequel): The Story of the Little Red
Box